Life
is What
Matters

Life is What Matters

It's time to be happy again

ALKA DIXIT

Srishti
PUBLISHERS & DISTRIBUTORS

SRISHTI PUBLISHERS & DISTRIBUTORS
Registered Office: N-16, C.R. Park
New Delhi – 110 019
Corporate Office: 212A, Peacock Lane
Shahpur Jat, New Delhi – 110 049
editorial@srishtipublishers.com

First published by
Srishti Publishers & Distributors in 2018

Printed at Repro Knowledgecast Limited, Thane

To my parents, who always guide me,
Prakash, who believes in my beliefs,
and
Rahil and Adit,
who made me complete.

Contents

Acknowledgement	*ix*
Preface	*xi*
Part A: Your Life is your Kid	1
Part B: Other Factors beyond Control	90
Part C: Odds of Life	109
An End is a New Beginning	147
References	*149*

Acknowledgement

As I complete this book, I really feel overwhelmed by the encouragement and appreciation I got from many precious people in my life.

To begin with, there were many people who knew from the beginning about the book and gave me enough inspiration, motivation and guidance throughout the process.

First of all, I express my sincere gratitude to my father, N.L.Dixit, for guiding and giving valuable inputs; and my mother, Raj Dixit, for being a continuous support and guide.

To my husband Prakash, for believing in my beliefs and for extending his helping hand, always. You are my strength.

This book could never be a possibility had Rahil and Adit not understood that their mom needed 'time to write'. I love you, and you know that nothing is more important to me.

To Jitin Dixit, whose memories are still fresh in my mind, and who still influences my life despite not being there for years.

I would like to convey my special thanks to Nilisha Dixit, Dr Sunita Gupta, Dr Nitika Anand and Dr Rekha Sharma, who read the evolving script and offered advice. Because of their help, I am content with the final result. This would never be a possibility without their valuable inputs.

To my closest friends Sunita, Anurita and Archana for accepting me the way I am and still having me in their lives. I cherish our friendship.

I sincerely thank you all precious people from the family and friends for encouraging me throughout the process. I may not be able to include your name here, but you all know that your name is engraved in my heart. You all helped me to evolve as a person and as a human being.

Last but not the least, I am really grateful to the editorial and publishing team of Srishti Publishers who took enough pains to work on every aspect of the book, thus making this book a visual treat.

Thank you all for your extraordinary support and love!

Preface

Edit your life frequently and ruthlessly. It's your masterpiece, after all.

Before you start reading this book, let me make it clear that I'm not a 'guru', nor am I claiming through this book that I know anything more than you do. No, I'm not. The simple reason for writing this book is to share some of my experiences with you, which I think can help some of you. And I believe that if any of you benefit by this book, then the purpose of this book would be fulfilled.

Though this book can be helpful for any person with any kind of problem, I personally feel that people of the following three categories may find this book exceptionally helpful:

1. THOSE DEALING WITH ANXIETY AND DEPRESSION

Depression and anxiety raising its head in my mind, distrust, disbelief, anger in my heart and ocean of tears in my eyes, all were enough to put a noose around my neck.

Suicide is a major threat in society today. Unfortunately, it can be seen across all age groups and socioeconomic sections. The life which one should live with dignity seems just like a toy for some. They are ready to give it up without giving it a second thought, either by committing suicide or by losing interest in their lives completely, which, in my view, is no less than suicide.

Why do people take their lives for granted? It is because they don't value it. They don't realize that this is the only life they have got on this earth, and instead of living it to the fullest, they waste it for trivial reasons.

On the other hand, there are people whose lives are full of struggles from the beginning; yet they know the value of every single moment of their lives. They know how to live it to the fullest, and how to make the most out of whatever they have. Through this book, I'll share with you some inspiring stories of such people.

2. THOSE WHO HAVE SACRIFICED THEIR LIVES

This category belongs to all those who give up a bit of themselves for others, and more specifically, the beautiful ladies out there.

She could be anyone; she is you, she is me and she is her too. She can be your mom, your aunt, your wife, your sister, just about anyone.

Ever wondered what all these ladies have in common? They have all sacrificed their lives for the sake of their families. They have put their families first, and their own lives behind. I am not saying that there is something wrong in it. No, it's not that at all.

To raise kids, to do household chores, to take care of one's family, to balance a professional life with the personal – those are sacred tasks which can be done by a pious heart of a mother and a wife only. The only thing I want to say through this book is that what if we take care of our lives just as well. What if we raise both our kids and our own life simultaneously? Sounds better, right?

3. ALL OF US

Yes, you read it right. All of us in our life journeys have felt depressed at least once, and have also sacrificed our lives for someone we love and care for. So this book, very truly, belongs to all of us.

There are many people, and I have seen many women around me too, who are doing a lot of things simultaneously, to deal with their families, their work and their *own life*.

Through my son, I met Dr Aditi, who was given so little in her life, yet she has overcome all the hurdles with courage and perseverance. She has emerged like a winner from the sad story of her life by using a foolproof plan invented by her.

Life is What Matters is a book based on her ideology in her own words which teaches us to value our lives.

This is a self-help book which tells us to shift our thought process just to value our lives a bit more, because we live only once.

The basic aim of this plan is to prepare the readers in a way that they think about their lives with empathy and give it due respect and importance.

"If I ask you, what do you love most in your life, what would you say?" Dr Aditi asked me that day when we both were discussing about the ups and downs of life.

"Well, my kids, without any doubt," I answered in a flash of a second.

"I bet that more than 90% people will say this and they'll tell me a hundred reasons for the same," she agreed with me. "What if I ask you to love your life in the same way?" she asked me the second question. I was short of words as I started imagining my life, like my very own child. I wondered how my life would be different if I followed this idea.

"What a brilliant idea, Aditi!" I said with hope and excitement in my voice.

"Yes! See, I consider myself mother of two rather than one – my son, Aarav, and my life," she continued. "That way I give equal importance to both."

"But how do you do that?" I asked.

"Well, I deal with my life the same way I deal with Aarav, my son. By the way, how can I explain everything right here? Let's meet again and discuss this in detail," she said with the familiar smiling face.

As I could not wait any longer to learn more about this idea, we set a meeting for the very next day. I was intrigued by what she had told me.

And that forms the core idea of this plan: *to presume that your life is your kid and treat it just the way you treat your child.*

The next day, I reached her house before time and she narrated her life story and the core idea of this plan which simply means that you have to give the same importance and weightage to your life as you give to your child.

This is, indeed, a very interesting aspect of this plan, *to treat your life just the way you treat your child.* You need so much compassion, empathy, along with strictness and certain rules to deal with it. It is as simple as that. If you look at that perspective, then you'll realize that there is a lot of similarity between your life and your kid. Both need to be taken care of, to be dealt with compassion and at times with strictness too. You'll also realize that you can't run away from them because they are the most important parts of your existence and you have enormous responsibility towards them.

So when you think your life is your child, you instantly feel responsible towards it. And it becomes your duty to give one hundred percent towards your life to make it worth living. Most of the time people tell us that they are a victim of their destiny, but in reality, we try to take our lives for granted by saying so. In other words, we run away from the responsibilities we have towards our own life.

According to Dr Aditi, if you presume that your life is your baby, you will be able to find answers to the three most important aspects of your life:

1. How to love your life again?
2. How to streamline your life's activities?
3. How to fulfill its dreams?

Now you can see that the most important part of this plan is to 'love your life' the same way you love your child, and it becomes much more important to do so with your life. Why? Well, with your child, it's a bilateral relationship, and you along with your child will be equally responsible for his / her life which can turn out to be successful or not so successful.

But it's not the same with your life, because you are in a unilateral relationship with your life. You are the only active participant, so it's you, only you, who are responsible for a good or miserable life. So again, I'll say that love your child, and love your life even more. Because when you love your life, you'll love yourself; and when you love yourself, then only can you love others.

The next important thing is, 'how to streamline your life and how to control your life's activities'. There may be positive or negative aspects of your life, but when they are unplanned or uncontrolled, they will only clutter your life. Even positive vibes may not be able to regain the charm of your life.

So, at what time should you turn your life to get a more fulfilled living which gives you the happiness you are craving for?

That time is *now,* and let me tell you that this is not impossible at all. Through others and my own life journey, I have observed and researched many things which happened either for the good or bad. And all the experiences I gained have helped me to make a foolproof plan which can change your life for the better.

The last most important aspect of life is 'to fulfill your life's dream' and this is the most interesting part of the plan. I have read somewhere that one should have three hobbies.

One hobby is to *earn*.

The second hobby to keep yourself *fit*.

And the last one is *creativity*.

So you tell me, how many of these hobbies do you have? Because it is these hobbies and interests that most of our life's dreams are linked to.

In a nutshell, following things will come to your mind as soon as you presume that 'Your Life is Your Kid.' And that gives you the 'Rule of Three' which includes three important aspects of your life:

Your life is your kid

Happiness of your kid (Life here)

Love it

Streamline it

Fulfil its dreams

Part A:
Your Life is your Kid

Introduction

Life is What Matters is the story of a girl who achieved almost everything that she wanted in life. It's her way of living that leads her to the path where life is extremely easy to live and beautiful to see. And it was not easy. It took her prime years with a lot of hard work and perseverance to build a plan which is so easy to execute and so effective. Her life motivates me to write her story in a form of a proper plan told to me by the girl herself.

"Arya, fast, we are getting late," I shouted from the kitchen as I was preparing lunch for my hubby Nikhil, who was about to leave for office.

"Mom, tell me what I am supposed to wear," Arya shouted from his room.

'Uff, when will this boy grow up!' I spoke to myself. 'Today is his parent-teacher meeting and I need to talk to his class teacher, but it seems we are already late.'

I went into Arya's room and helped him get ready. After which I again rushed back to the kitchen and packed lunch for Nikhil.

After finishing all the morning household chores, it took me another thirty minutes to get ready. Thankfully, Nikhil agreed to drop us to the school. We somehow managed to reach there on time. In the midst of this confusion and stress, I didn't even look at myself in the mirror. I managed to make myself presentable in the car itself, and that seemed more than enough for me. We rushed to his class and joined the other parents and students waiting for their turn to come.

'I don't remember if I switched off the lights before locking the house. What will Arya's teacher tell me about his studies? I was thinking of discussing something about him, but I forgot what that was. Nikhil must have reached office by now. He hasn't even informed me. So careless he is!'

I was surrounded by clouds of thoughts and was feeling somewhat stressed due to the overdose of my thoughts and speculations. And that was when I noticed her.

She was sitting in the opposite corner of the class and quite far from me, but something in her personality prevented me from moving my eyes away from her. She was not beautiful in the conventional sense of the word, but an aura of tranquility was so obvious that I was in awe of her charm. Not just me, but I could notice many eyes gazing at her. Her fair complexion was radiating a bright hue of hope against her black sari. Her white steel watch merged nicely with her clean skin tone. She must have been around thirty, short and plump, but her smiling face was truly charming. She looked calm, happy and comfortable in her own skin and that might have been the reason that she looked so attractive. I instantly felt the need to go to her and introduce myself.

"Arya!" I heard his teacher's voice.

'Oh no, it seems our turn has come.' I thought and was really disappointed. By the time we finished the meeting and other formalities, she had already left. Later I asked Arya about her, but he could not recall her.

Days passed and I moved on in the rattle race of life, but her image somewhere stuck in my mind. In the forthcoming parent-teacher meeting, I tried to look for her again, but in vain.

One day Arya insisted that he wanted to see his friend Aarav. I refused as I had too much work at hand that day. Moreover, I felt a little uncomfortable as I didn't know his parents. But he told me that he had to do some common group activity given by his class teacher on a project he was deeply involved in, and hence I had to make time. I agreed when he insisted. I knew it was his dream project and he was quite serious about it.

On the way to Aarav's home, I asked about his parents.

"His father is a doctor," Arya told me.

"Ok, and what about his mother?" I asked.

"Oh aunty! She is very nice. We like her a lot," he replied with an affectionate smile on his face.

"What sort of an answer is that! I'm asking about her profession," I said in an annoyed tone.

"Aarav told me once that she works for the needy ones. What do we call them, Mom?" he asked.

"Oh, so she is a social worker!" I answered.

"Yes, social worker," Arya shouted. "Aarav told me that she does many things and I think she is a doctor too, but I'm not sure," Arya murmured.

My curiosity was on a big high by now. I definitely wanted to see that lady after the description given by Arya. His smile showed clearly how fond of her he was! In another fifteen minutes, we reached their house.

It was not a very big house and looked quite simple from the outside. However, It was artistically beautiful inside, with indoor plants, unique showpieces, paintings and so on. When we entered the house, the maid guided us to the drawing room, where Aarav's mother was already sitting surrounded by six or seven ladies. The drawing room was simple as well, with only a few pieces of furniture and few decorative items.

"Namaste Aunty," Aarav greeted me with a smile.

"Namaste beta," I answered and looked at Arya expecting the same from him. Arya did not take much time and greeted Aarav's mother. She turned towards Arya with a smile on her face.

'Oh my god, she is the same gorgeous lady I was dying to see!' I muttered in my mind.

I was extremely happy to be there at that moment, and for that, I thanked Arya again and again in my mind.

She was in a blue cotton sari with her loose straight hair falling on her shoulders. Her sitting posture was so elegant that she really looked like a diva. As soon as she looked at us, she welcomed us and I could feel the warmth in her gesture. I was completely mesmerized by her attitude, her way of talking and empathy towards everyone.

Later I got to know that she was a practicing doctor. We instantly liked each other's company and from then on, started chatting over the phone regularly. She was so full of life, always smiling and teeming with positive thoughts all the time. After some time I got to know that she was well liked by many people in our vicinity too. She was popular on social media, not as a doctor, but as a person. Many of our common friends told me that they discussed their problems with her because they got concrete solutions most of the time. I realized that not only me, but many people liked her as a person and saw her as their ideal and wanted to become like her. She was not the most intelligent, successful or beautiful person on earth, if you look at it the conventional way, but her attitude towards life made her so. She looked very calm and content and that reflected in her beauty and body language. In fact, she looked beautiful because of her calmness, contentment and almost always smiling face.

I didn't know if her life journey was as smooth as it looked and wondered if she ever faced any downfall in her life. I really wanted to know this, and for that, I needed to be in regular touch with her. So I decided to visit her place again. Arya agreed to accompany me. As soon as we reached, I eagerly waited to see her again. She came down in a white and pink suit with the usual smile on her face. Her overall personality seemed to be well kept and well groomed. An aura of calmness, contentment and positivity always seemed to ooze out of her, which I must say was quite infectious. I could feel that sense of positivity inside me too. It was really a treat to the senses to see her again. She welcomed us warmly in her familiar way.

We shared a lot about our lives and when I looked back into her life, I found that it had been a roller coaster ride for her. Only a really strong person could have dealt with such a turbulent life. I asked her the secret of staying calm in all those situations and to emerge like a winner with so much positivity all around. She just smiled. I wanted to persist so that she could open up a little bit, but I didn't, because I wanted to make her comfortable enough to share it on her own.

We met many times after that and she impressed me even more, every time she opened the layers of her personality. She had suffered so much in her life, but hats off to her to have made her life so special and beautiful out of the resources she had. She never complained about the miseries of her life, rather she was always smiling and helpful to others.

When I looked into the depth of her life, I found that during her childhood, she suffered a life-threatening infection, and though she survived, she was unfortunately left with some permanent deformities. That resulted in an abnormal person who was born perfectly normal.

If I honestly compare my life before I met her and after that, I must say that it has changed dramatically. It's not like something miraculous has happened, but it has changed due to the change in my attitude. I have learnt to make my life fulfilling by following her path, which is so generous and open to everyone who wants to follow it.

Now I find myself more content, peaceful, calm and happy.

If we look deep into life's purpose, then it is contentment, satisfaction and happiness that we seek. I realized that if I could find these rarities through this path, then many more people can. So I decided to write a book about it and take it as a project which includes both me and Dr Aditi.

I discussed this with Dr Aditi, and she just laughed at my idea. But when I told her that I was serious, she readily agreed. After that we had regular meetings, where she narrated her life experiences to me.

What she told me has been taken up as a project to benefit everyone in the form of this book. This book is written to elaborate the secret to happiness in her life, in her own words.

The secret revealed by her is:

'I consider my life as my kid, and to make this kid successful and for it to blossom like a flower, I only look for these three components:

1. I need to love my child (here, life)
2. I need to streamline its regular and special activities
3. I need to fulfill my kid's (here, life) dream.'

YOUR LIFE IS YOUR KID

> *I found that if you love life, life will love you back.*
> *– Arthur Robinstein*

"Ma'am, I'm telling you, she cannot do better than this. She doesn't have that caliber. Look at her handwriting! She can't even write properly; she only scribbles," said her class teacher in an annoyed tone. The third grader in a pink and white frock was trying to understand the reason of her annoyance. She looked at her mom who looked embarrassed and then at her teacher who still looked annoyed and irritated. The poor girl was quiet, but scared, as she could make out something wrong in the conversation. Her mom said nothing to her, but took permission from her teacher to leave the class. On their way back home, her mom kept mum, although looking disturbed.

As soon as they reached home, her mom got onto some household work and she started playing with her brother and infant sister. The fear she had felt till then, had vanished and she seemed happy in her cocoon with her siblings. That is the beauty of a child's innocence. They forget everything so quickly and so easily. After a while, her mom called her up.

She entered the room and saw her mom sitting there. Her mom still looked disturbed. She asked the little girl about her school in detail as she was trying to find out the cause of her poor performance in the class. I am not sure if the little girl was able to put her point across to her mother, but her mother very clearly explained a few things to her:

1. Education is very important for everyone. In fact, it is the easiest way to earn money and survive comfortably in this world.
2. Moreover, education is all the more important for a person who is not fortunate enough to survive *normally* in this world.

The little girl clearly understood that she had to study harder, and she did exactly that. In the next class test, she was able to score more than ninety percent. Everyone, including her parents and class teacher, was surprised to see the improvement in her performance.

A few years passed by and now that little girl was a thirteen-year-old teenager. She was a brilliant student. She had made up her mind from the beginning that despite her limitations, she had to survive and be an achiever. She had faced all sorts of bullying, but that was another story. People used to ignore and overlook her needs and she herself started believing that because of her deformity, she did not deserve good things in life. So much so that she had almost accepted this fate, and that too happily. However, she had faith in god and never doubted his plans for her life. And that was reason enough to make her go.

Years passed by, things changed, and she grew up into a docile, not so confident girl. She could hardly say no to anyone, as if she had done something wrong . Her confidence levels were so low that she believed anyone who was just about talking to her, was staring, and that made her self-conscious too. Those who tried to know her were nice to her, while the rest of the world hardly noticed her.

At such a young age, when kids were busy playing and enjoying life, she was struggling to be accepted by others. Through all the years, she concluded one thing – she has to love and accept herself unconditionally first, and only then will the others accept her. She did the same and now you can see the result.

"That little girl was me," said Dr Aditi.

At that point I insisted that Dr Aditi tells me her life story in detail, and she agreed.

A LIFE BEYOND ORDINARY

I am from a very small town of India, where a girl child was considered more of a liability. Fortunately or unfortunately, I was the second daughter to my parents, so I was even more unwelcome in my family. I came to know later that my grandfather didn't even visit me when I was born as he was expecting a grandson. To add to that, two things happened in my childhood, which further determined my destiny.

First, when I was two years old, my younger brother was born and all the attention and care turned towards the newly born baby, which was natural too. But because I was also very young, I couldn't get the much needed affection and love at that tender age.

Secondly, due to negligence or some other reason, I contracted Tuberculosis of the spinal vertebrae. Being a child, it was difficult to diagnose it, and much more difficult to treat. It was the old times and treatment facilities were not up to the mark, so it took a very long time to heal the infection. And though the healing gradually happened, unfortunately, it left behind some unwanted consequences.

When I was young, I couldn't feel any discrimination because it was easier to live under the loving shadow of my family and I'm really thankful for everything my parents did for all of us siblings, be it education, values, freedom, etc.; we got everything in optimal doses. But as I grew, I started feeling that I was not a normal child. Though I must admit here that despite all these things, my childhood was completely normal, and thanks to my parents and siblings for that. They always encouraged me and enhanced my confidence, no matter what.

But the real problem was to deal with the outer world. The world which was full of beautiful and charming kids never acknowledged my existence. I used to see girls chatting and playing with their friends, completely ignoring me. I tried hard to get their attention, but it was not that easy to break into their zone.

And back at home, things were not any better. Though my family always supported me, I was a great source of worry for my parents. I overheard them many times discussing my future, marriage, career, etc.

Surprisingly, my grandfather who had been unhappy at my birth now started liking me. I don't know why, but maybe because of my nature and personality which I developed according to others' needs to please them. I used to say and do things to please others. *I created importance for myself by giving importance to others.* I won't say that it was wrong, but in the process, I forgot to live on my own terms. There were some changes in my attitude too. I became more jovial with a great sense of humour and my classmates now started liking my company. Also, I was a completely harmless soul, so they used to feel comfortable in my company.

I remember one of my friends saying that I was just like *jaggery* that attracts so many flies around it and we used to laugh over that.

In the journey of life, I met many people and I will say that ninety percent, in fact, more, were good. But this is also true that most of the time I was the one who initiated any relationship, only then they would come forward.

The major change came in my life when I went to the hostel. I met a lot of people from different cultures with different attitudes. That was the period of life where I made true friends who really helped me boost my confidence. I really enjoyed that phase of life which helped me grow into the woman I am today.

I admit that it was not an easy journey, but through all ups and downs of life, I learned that life goes on. It flows like an unstoppable river, in all directions, with all force; sometimes slow, very slow, and sometimes so fast, as if it does not have time to look around or look back even for a moment. Whether we like it or not, this is what life really teaches us. Lessons we learn from life are enormous and not easy, but we grow in the wisdom of life with each one.

After completing my MBBS and MD, I was advised to get married and get settled. My parents were really worried about my marriage. I had two younger siblings who were studying and their responsibility was on their shoulders as well.

I had decided that in order to live happily, I needed to be independent first. I had just finished my medical education, so I started looking for a job. In the meantime, I also started preparing for the civil services examination as I wanted to opt for the highest job of the country. However, I couldn't pursue that further as I got married before the examinations itself. It's not that my husband or in-laws didn't want me to appear for it, but it was my state of mind. I decided not to pursue it and instead started working as a Medical Officer. And till date, I regret the fact that I didn't pursue that dream of mine.

This taught me one thing – no matter how many obstacles come into your life, you should never give up on your dreams and passions.

Believe me, your dreams are meant to come true, and only you yourself are not letting them happen.

After I got married, I got busy in the rattle race of life with added responsibilities.

If I look back, I remember so many things said to me to discourage me, but I was determined to prove them wrong. Though I won't say that I have achieved something big in life, but this is also true that whatever I've indeed achieved, has been against all odds. And for that, I can't thank god enough. I believe that I'm his dearest child and my faith in him keeps me going through all the ups and downs.

1. **They said that I would not survive, and I am very much alive.** A girl child was considered a burden to the family due to the dowry system back then. Sadly this thinking still prevails in some parts of India. Though my parents never felt that way, but my grandparents somewhere still had that at the back of their mind. A child without love and affection can never grow in the normal way. Moreover, I contracted Tuberculosis which was considered a deadly disease in those time. At one point of time, everyone thought that my survival is impossible, but I survived. I not only survived, but fought every obstacle and am still very much alive.

2. **They said I may not live an ordinary life, so I lived an extraordinary one**. My parents were told that I may not be able to live like other children, due to the deadly infection. And the doctors were right in a way, because I developed permanent deformity of the spine and my life turned upside down. My childhood, adolescence, and youth, everything was completely changed due to that. But still, I survived normally because *I perceived everything that happened to me as normal*. I never demanded anything or expected anything beyond that and that may be the reason I survived almost normally

even after that. Though it is all normal in my perspective, but for others, I may be living an extraordinary life as they never expected me to become what I am today.

3. **They said I won't be able to walk, so I ran.** Even after that, things were not better. As my spine was severely affected by the infection, doctors feared that my lower body may not be able to bear my weight. In simpler words, they were not sure if I could be able to walk on my feet. I really want to thank them for their visionary approach and for smelling the coffee in the beginning itself. Had doctors shown a little negligence, their fear might have become a truth.

   Though they were not sure about my existence, but my god always was. I started walking and even running normally despite all my reports showing that I cannot walk.

4. **They said I could not compete with my peer group, and I topped the school.** Then there were real challenges in terms of starting my studies. Today I understand the value of a normal childhood. Half of my childhood was gone in the treatment of my illness. So a big challenge was to compete with my peer group. However, education was the only thing in my life where I consider myself really blessed. I was a bright student from the beginning, and even after all those setbacks, I was at par with the others. Though it was also true that I used to miss playing with my friends and siblings. A normal routine by others' standards was missing in life, but I started accepting all those hospital appointments

as a part of my life. I started finding happiness in all those smelly corridors of hospitals. Then I started my studies to finish them at a normal pace. And later, with the blessing of god, I topped in academics many times during my school days.

5. **They said I could not complete my MBBS, but I completed my MD too**. I still remember the very first day in the medical college when one of my teachers came and asked me if I would be able to do my laboratory work, as according to her, I was too short to reach the table. She might have been right in her views, but thankfully, I never gave her a heed and that is the reason I could finish my graduation and later also pursued my post-graduation.

Despite all these setbacks in my life, I never complained about anything.

From all the good and bad experiences of life, it so happens that some people choose only the bad ones and make their and others' lives miserable. On the other hand, some people see only positivity in life, even if their life is full of struggles. They try to make themselves as well as others happy. These kind of people have complete control over their lives. It doesn't mean that they have very rigid and set rules for life, but they treat their life just 'like their child'. That they are in complete love with their lives and they know exactly when to control and when to let go in life.

Many times I heard people saying that 'my child is my life'. What if we say vice versa? As in, how does it feel if we say that my life is my child? It may seem very simple, but it really has a very deep meaning to it.

So, it would be a better idea if we treat our life just like our kids. But before we go any further, let's see some similarities between the two:

1. You can't have many complaints about your kid as well as from life. In other words, you have to accept them as they are.
2. Both may go out of control at times and it may become really difficult to bring them back on track again.
3. You can nurture your life the same way that you nurture your kids.
4. You have to appreciate whatever you get from your life and just forget and forgive what you don't, as you do with your kids.
5. You can shape your life, just like your kids.
6. You can be liberal with them sometimes and strict at others.
7. You cannot compare your life to others because just like every child, every life is unique.
8. You know what is best for your life, just as you know about your kids.
9. Your life, like your kid, is *your* responsibility and not others'.
10. Your life and your kid are inseparable parts of you and *you* are the reason for their existence.

These are a few striking similarities between the two. You can add on many if you think deeply about it.

When you love your life, you have complete control over your life and you will never see life as a problem or burden. It is your life, so it is what you make of it, out of the resources available to you. We have this tendency to blame others for our unhappy life. But if you look deep down, this is not true, because 'life' is a very individual and unique thing. So it's only 'you' who is responsible for its outcome. You can make it or you can waste it. And to waste it like that or to take it for granted may result in a miserable life.

So we need a complete balance to deal with our lives, just as we need with our child. Those who have kids may understand this better. But those who don't have kids may imagine how they will treat their child if they had one. We need to treat our lives in the same manner. Sometimes we need to show compassion, sometimes craziness, sometimes strictness and yes, sometimes we need to even punish it if it goes wrong.

The other important thing to realize here is that as your child takes birth from you and is a part of you, the same way your life is a part of you; it derives from you only. All the basic needs of your life as well as your child depend on your existence. So *your* happiness, unhappiness or stress may ultimately shape your life.

At this point, we should understand that all the problems life imparts are actually our expectations from life. More expectations, more stress. The very simple point here is that if you have expectations from your kid and your life, you are having too many expectations from yourself. *You* instantly become the root cause of all problems and *you* are the only one who has all the tools to solve the problems too. So *you* become the cause of all the problems as well as the solution. In other words, you are just playing with yourself and your life, wasting your time and at the end gaining nothing. So if you are not getting anything out of it, why do you need to enter into such a *chakravyuh* to make your life hard to live and harder to love.

The other aspect is why we need to look at our life in that perspective? Why compare it with my child and why not with certain others, for instance, the parents? Well, the answer to this is very simple and I want to say it in a few points:

1. You never feel that empathy and compassion towards your parents as you feel towards your child.
2. You never feel that responsible towards your parents as you feel towards your child because your child is completely dependent on you till a certain age.
3. You can't be strict and can never punish your parents for their mistakes.
4. Your life and your child derived from you, not your parents.

Can you see now? Empathy, compassion, responsibility, strictness, ownership, etc., all are important ingredients to love your life, to control it and to make it worth living.

ACTION PLAN

A. How to Love Your Life?
I. A Big Nod

> *My happiness grows in direct proportion to my acceptance, and in inverse proportion to my expectations.*
> *– Michael J. Fox*

The first and foremost important step towards this plan is to accept your life as it is, the way you unconditionally accept your child.

It could be the worst phase of your life; any unsuccessful event or any other disappointment. Whatever it is, just accept it. That is the only key towards a better life.

So how does it work?

When you accept your life despite all the setbacks, you immediately become at peace with yourself and your life. This results in a state of calmness which leads to less worrying and more control over the situation. Initially, it may not result in satisfaction, but this state of mind is enough to de-stress you from all the negative thoughts of the past.

As Robert Holden puts it in his book *Happiness Now!*, 'Happiness and self-acceptance go hand in hand. In fact, your level of self-acceptance determines your level of happiness. The more self-acceptance you have, the more happiness you'll allow yourself to accept, receive and enjoy. In other words, you enjoy as much happiness *as you believe you're worthy of.*'

In order to accept your life, you have to accept yourself first.

A few days back, while I was on my way to my clinic, I came across a young, handsome man. As I was at a distance, I could see only his good physique and smiling face. He was sitting and coming towards me, so I could make out that he was sitting on a wheelchair. As he came nearer, I was literally shocked to see that both his legs were amputated from above the knee. I couldn't believe my eyes. A young, handsome boy who had met with such a tragic accident and was still smiling? But that's what happens to some unfortunate people owing to the cruel hands of destiny. Though I wanted to talk to him, I could not gather enough courage at that time.

The very next day I asked about him to my nursing staff and came to know that he had lost both his legs in a road accident. I decided to talk to him to evaluate his mental status after what he had gone through.

While entering his room, I was experiencing mixed feelings of hesitation as well as grief. Then there he was, smiling again, sitting with his mother. I could see definite worry in his mother's eyes, but not in his.

I started a conversation with a few casual questions as I wanted to assess his mental status, but at the same time didn't want to hurt him. To my surprise, he answered all the questions with confidence and seemed at ease with himself. Then I came to the point, "It's really very unfortunate that you had such a tragic accident, and….?" I was short of words.

He just smiled a little and said, "Well, I lost both my legs a few days ago. It was a tragic accident as you said, and unfortunately, I could do nothing to save my legs. My life is going to change completely as my legs were a part of my body, a part of me. But now that it has happened, I have to accept it. I've lost my legs, but a major part of my body is still with me and I'm happy for whatever I am left with. It could have been worse. I could have lost my hands too, my senses, anything could have gone. *But my dignity, my senses, my wholeness as a person to live my life, all that is still with me.* I'm very much the same person as long as people make me feel so. It's just as if some part of me is missing and I have to learn to live without it. Though I know that my life will not be the same now and I have to face challenges as well, but *as long as I am in love with myself, I'm ready to face everything.*"

I could not say anything for a few minutes. There was deep silence in the room and I could feel the warmth of rays of hope coming from his words. I just said, "God bless you." He just smiled back.

I rushed towards the door to hide my tears. The lesson he gave me was quite simple:

'Unconditional love and acceptance of yourself, despite all odds, is the key towards a fulfilling life.'

Now the question is, is there any technique to start accepting yourself? The answer is, *yes,* very much. But before that you need to look deep within yourself to find out the qualities you admire and you hate in yourself. If you think that you have no or minimal flaws in you and you can accept yourself the way you are, then nothing like it. And let me tell you that this is the true meaning of acceptance too.

But many times it happens that we don't like something about us and want to become like some other person we admire. If it is so, then believe me that most of the people are like that and we can follow the below mentioned technique to achieve the goal of changing ourselves for the better.

The technique is very simple and it needs only a few steps to transform you into a better version of you.

1. Shifting of thoughts.
2. Make a positive image of yourself.
3. Compare this image with the real you.
4. Do mark the differences between the two.
5. Try to work on the differences.
6. Can't do much? Ignore the rest.
7. Refuse to accept.
8. More chances of improvisation? Go ahead!
9. Accept the new you.
10. Love yourself unconditionally.

You can start this ten-step process to accept and love yourself unconditionally. Let's look at them one by one:

1. Shifting of thoughts

You may ask what exactly is the meaning of shifting of thoughts or thought shift? But before its proper meaning, let's start with the *willingness* to do that. Be willing to start a project, and when you decide on something, half the battle is won. Your decision is itself a sort of thought shift.

By shifting of thoughts we simply mean that a positive thought should overcome all your negative thoughts. When you decide that you have to start this plan, it reflects your willingness to get into a better life. This results in a positive impact as whatever you want to do is for a better life. It's that missing part of your life which you don't possess at this moment, but have been craving for long. And you know that if your wants/desires are strong enough, they will definitely be heard and be fulfilled.

2. Make a positive image of yourself

Well, here is a twist. I don't mean to make an image with the resources you have, instead, I mean to draw a big picture of you with or without all your resources.

What do you want to do?

What do you want to look like?

What do you like in others?

Who is your ideal?

What do you want from life?

These are a few questions which you need to ask yourself to build that positive image. Think as far as you can and make that image even if it turns out to be completely different from yourself.

Think in detail about everything: your looks, your apparel, accessories, body language, your manners, your house, your communication skills; anything. Think as vividly as you can.

Now look closely at this image. Do you love your transformation? Anything which you want to add or deduct, do it now.

Give a final touch and voila, you are done. Try to save as many copies of this new you in your mind, PC, papers, notebook, wherever it is possible to save.

3. Compare this image with the real you

Now, here comes the real test. You have an improved version of you, so now you have to compare it with the real you. What are the things that are missing or exceeding in you?

Make reasonable and practical goals for yourself, because while making a positive image, you might not look rationally into it. So this is the time to think rationally about it.

4. Do mark the differences between the two

Now you can clearly see the differences between your positive image and the real you.

Again, you may cut short a few things which you think may not be necessary or are not worth including.

5. Try to work on the differences

Can you apply or deduct these differences?
- If yes, then how? Make a list of total expenditures, time consumption, manpower, research, etc., which you may require during your transformation.
- If your answer is a no, then why is it so? What are the hurdles which stop you from achieving your goals? Can you remove some of them?

If you need some help from your family and friends here (manpower), try to get it.

6. Can't do much? Ignore the rest

Do whatever you can to make your goal possible. But after a lot of hard work and with all your resources, if you are still not getting a hundred percent, then leave the rest. Ignore it completely and forget about it.

If I am saying forget about it, then you have to literally forget the rest, otherwise you may not be able to accept yourself completely.

7. Refuse to accept

Well, this is a paradox. When we are talking about acceptance, why should we refuse to accept?

This is very simple because we are talking about 'negativity' here. All negative thoughts as well as any ill feeling coming to your mind should be refused to be entertained from the beginning itself. You are worried about something, say aloud that it's not going to happen at all and it won't happen in reality too. Accept only positivity from your updated image and reject all the negativity that is stressful for you.

8. More chances of improvisation? Go ahead

Again, make your image after all the updates. Okay, so this is your image with everything that you have.

How do you feel?

Happy?

Not so happy?

If you think at this point that you are still lacking something, then go ahead! Just remember one thing: nothing can stop you until you get your desired image. Make your last effort and see a completely new you.

9. Accept the new you

With all your efforts and ideas to put into yourself, here you are, with an ideal and better version of you to adore and admire. You have got what you have longed for.

10. Love yourself unconditionally

So you have seen how you can accept and love yourself unconditionally after working on it. And if you can't work on it due to any reason, then you need not worry. Just continue to accept and love yourself the way you are, because *no one on earth can play your role better than you.* So play your role well and always be there to applaud your efforts, irrespective of what others say.

II. Less is Plenty

Less needs, less worries!

When I wanted to get married, I only needed one guy. When I wanted to have kids, I only needed to have one or two. When I wanted to have good friends, I only needed one or two friends. I only needed one home to live in, and so on…

Can you see here? *We always worry in our life in a very disproportionate way. What we need is not much, but we worry a lot* about getting it. We only need one wonderful life partner, one or two kids, one house, one or two cars and that's about it. Is it too much to ask for? No, it's not.

Then why do we spend the whole of our life in worrying just to get this much! The day you start thinking whether in the whole world, you can't even get one Mr Right for yourself, you will become stress free at once. And that's true for every decision of your life. *What you want will be given to you in the same amount that you need.*

What I mean to say here is that as humans, we all need very little to survive, but our desires to get more and more are the reasons for our stress and unhappiness.

To limit our desires is the key to lead a successful life.

When I was still studying in the medical college, my parents started to look for a suitable boy for me. They searched a lot, but couldn't get the one. They were tensed, but I wasn't, for I knew that someone somewhere was surely waiting for me. And yes, I was right. I got married to a wonderful guy in no time.

So the simple idea is to 'minimize your needs and thus minimize your worries'.

And this philosophy works in every field of life.

But, one word of caution here. The purpose of the whole universe is to conspire to provide you with your needs or desire, but to keep and maintain that precious thing in your life is solely your responsibility. How to keep it with you throughout your life is solely your passion and hard work. So don't think that by changing merely your thought process, you can do something; it's all about perseverance and the hard work you do, and that will change your life.

Now the one pivotal question here is that what if you don't get even that minimal need? It happens with many people that they don't get their smallest need fulfilled, forget about the desires. So what should be your mode of action in that scenario? The answer here is not easy as a lot of pain or suffering in the form of depression or feeling of worthlessness may surface.

But, what you can do here simply can be divided into two paths:

– Passive

– Active

I'll take passive first as it shows that you have to do nothing, simply wait and watch. Maybe your time still hasn't come, so just relax for the time being. If you are financially strong enough, then yes, you can utilize this time to rejuvenate your thought process. It can be done in any form – a vacation, a short trip to your old school, a spa, a nature walk – and you'll have a lot of benefit from this:

1. You'll feel rejuvenated, so you can think better.
2. You might have met other people and can realize that their lives are even more challenging.
3. You can learn from them that struggle is a part of life.
4. You can learn to smile in despair.
5. You can learn to deal with setbacks without any complaints
6. You can surely learn to manage your life in a more organized way.
7. You can have more mental, emotional and physical energy to do everyday things.
8. By giving yourself time, you'll see your life and your problems in retrospect and may come up with some better ideas to solve them.
9. You can introspect about yourself and your present situation.
10. You can now easily visualize what you actually want from life.

It's always better to go for a short trip when you have lost the sight of the path you are travelling on.

The other plan is more important as it is an active plan and you have to take it up in an emergency situation.

The idea is very simple – you have to look deep into your life and see if there is anything you are left with. If yes, then you are lucky enough, and believe me, we all are lucky as we can always find that 'something' in our life with which we can work and bounce back to live our life accordingly. I know it may be a very difficult phase of your life, but the action plan you choose can streamline your life and make it more accommodating.

For example, you are in a relationship with someone, but due to some reason you can't marry that person and instead have to marry someone else. There are two problems here: one, you didn't get what you want, the other that you have to accept the one you don't want to. What will you do in this situation? Either you can mourn over what is gone (your love interest), or you can look up to your spouse, see his / her qualities, which can be much better than you might have ever imagined. Moreover, the other person might have never wanted to marry you in the first place.

So what is the better thing to do? Here, you need to apply the 'Active' plan, which means to move on with whatever you are left with, to make your life worth living, and as I said earlier, most of the times you are left with an enormous amount.

The simple idea here is to proportionate your worries with your needs. Don't worry too much for a simple thing, because once you get it, you won't value it in the same ratio. And this can further extend the worries, thus making it a never-ending process.

So what can you do to reduce your worries?

The answer is – count your blessings, be grateful and feel happy.

That's it!

III. Egg in One's Beer

A grateful heart is a magnet for miracles.

Once, I started counting my blessings, and I'm still going on…

I know you may have read about this many times, but believe me, your experience here is going to be quite different.

Everyone tells you to count your blessings, but very few might have told you how you do that. I'm going to tell you just that.

Blessings are those positive things in your life which you have longed for your whole life and which you really achieved after a lot of hard work. They may be anything, right from your education to your dream job, your spouse, your kids, just about anything.

The big question here is that who will decide blessings/positive factors of your life? You may say that obviously it's 'you' yourself. But many times it so happens that you, being in the situation, may not see your blessings clearly. But your real friends and family members sometimes may see that side of your life, which you might have been completely unaware of. So what are those steps through which you can identify all the positive factors of your life as well as your true potential?

Let's look at them one by one now:

1. The very first thing you need here is to have a heart to heart talk with yourself. Yes, this is the mandatory and very first step towards it.

2. By doing so you will come to know many things which may not be clear otherwise. So take a white sheet and note all these points. Note down everything coming to your mind as you can always edit the list later.

3. By having a conversation with yourself, many things will become clear. But still a lot of things remain about which you are ignorant, and for that, you should have a heart to heart talk with your spouse or close friend.

4. Now you have another list. Note this list down on that white sheet.

5. Till now you have a pretty good idea of all the blessings and positive things in your life.

6. At this point, if you are still not satisfied and want to talk to some other person, then go ahead as you can talk to as many people as you want and increase your list of blessings. The more, the merrier.

7. But, a word of caution here. This complete exercise is here just to plan your life in a way that you start loving your life and live a much more fulfilled life.

8. More positive factors may lead to an overconfident and egoistic you and if this happens, then the purpose of this book is completely lost.

9. So think about those blessings for which you really worked hard and which can instill a feel good factor in you rather than make you egoistic.

10. Count your blessings, feel good, enjoy your life, but at the same time, stay grounded.

Now you have an updated list of your blessings, your positive factors in life. Let me give you the examples of blessings which can help you prepare the list:

1. Good qualification
2. Understanding and loving parents
3. Caring family
4. Own house
5. Own vehicle
6. A satisfactory career
7. Understanding and caring spouse
8. Loving kids

9. Good looks and health
10. Strong support system in the form of friends and family
11. Better financial status
12. Dignified life
13. Sound mental status

These are a few basic examples and if you have them all, then I don't think that you have to worry at all. Then there are some minor things also which you can include in the list, like good clothes, a hobby, and so on.

Okay, so you have done that. Look at your list now. Are you impressed? Well print it out and paste it in your study. You are ready to go ☺

♌

It was an ordinary day, but something extraordinary happened that day. I was busy in my study writing a blog when I noticed a beautiful girl standing in the lane. She was around eighteen years old. Though she was standing quietly, I could make out that she was upset about something. I observed her for a few minutes and could see her sobbing in between. I couldn't stop myself and went to her. As she saw me coming towards her, she became conscious and tried to leave, but I went and said hello to her. She looked at me strangely, but said nothing. I smiled; she smiled back, though very shyly. I introduced myself and when she came to know that I was a doctor and a counsellor, she agreed to communicate. I asked her a few questions, to which she replied quietly. But one thing was very strange; after every answer, she used to add 'my hard luck'. I asked a few more things and got the same reply. Now I had come to know almost everything about her.

She was residing in the same colony. Her parents were separated and she was living with her mother and maternal grandparents. She had just passed her 10+2 and had taken admission in a reputed college in the same city. Within a few months of attending college, she got friendly with a guy. Just a few days back, that guy had proposed to her and they were a couple.

The previous day, she had a fight with her man and she was very upset that he had broken up with her for such a trivial reason. She told me how much she loved the guy and she could not survive without him.

I heard everything carefully and gave her my address and invited her to my place that evening. She agreed to come.

She arrived at five in the evening. We had tea and I don't know why, but she looked quite normal as if nothing had happened. I asked her the reason and got a strange answer. She told me that now she too didn't want to be with that guy. Instead, she would like to stay with her mom always. I understood immediately that this was a rebound phenomenon along with denial to accept the situation. And the wound was still there, which needed to be healed.

I held her hand; she tried to remain unfazed initially, but soon broke down. I did nothing and let her cry. Later, I gave her a few points to help her restart her life.

Three days after that, she came to my house with her mom. She was looking calm and balanced. Her mom thanked me for bringing her daughter out of that crisis.

Now, I'll tell you what I told the girl that evening:

1. You and your life are the first priority of your mom and your grandparents.
2. You *should be* your first priority too.
3. The guy actually doesn't belong to you, and if he does, then he is not a priority at all.
4. A guy who dares to leave you over a petty issue is not worthy of being in your life.
5. So shift your focus towards valuables in your life, like your mom, grandparents, your job, career and your friends.
6. And last but not the least, *think about yourself first.* Your happiness and peace are not important for that guy, but they should be important to you at least.

Friends, many times it happens that we give the authority of our life to another, who doesn't deserve that at all. Someone has said it so nicely, that when writing the story of your life, don't give the pen to someone else.

If you look carefully, then you can see hundreds of blessings in your life which are more than enough to make your life fulfilling. Just open your eyes and mind too, at least once!

Now, thanks to new research, there is scientific evidence that gratitude produces health benefits.

The research is summarized in Robert Emmons' new book *Thanks!: How the New Science of Gratitude Can Make You Happier* (Houghton Mifflin, 2007). Emmons and his colleagues at the University of California at Davis are among the pioneers in research on gratitude, part of a larger movement called positive psychology. Positive psychology, instead of focusing on illness and emotional problems, studies health-promoting behaviour and the pleasurable parts of life.

Emmons' book reports on several studies. In the first, he and his colleagues divided participants into three groups, each of which made weekly entries in a journal. One group wrote five things they were grateful for. Another group described five daily hassles and a control group listed five events that had affected them in some way. Those in the gratitude group felt better about their lives overall, were more optimistic about the future, and reported fewer health problems than the other participants. Results from a second study suggested that daily writing led to a greater increase in gratitude than a weekly practice.

A third study reproduced the results among a group of people suffering from various neuromuscular diseases, including post-polio syndrome, which has symptoms similar to those in CFS. People using daily gratitude journals reported more satisfaction with their lives and were more optimistic about the future than the control group. Interestingly, the gratitude group also reported getting more sleep, spending less time awake before falling asleep and feeling more refreshed in the morning.

In a related study, researchers at the University of Connecticut found that gratitude can have a protective effect against heart attacks. Studying people who had experienced one heart attack, the researchers found that those patients who saw benefits and gains from their heart attack, such as becoming more appreciative of life, experienced a lower risk of having another heart attack.

The research on gratitude challenges the idea of a 'set point' for happiness, a belief that just as our body has a set point for weight, each person may have a genetically-determined level of happiness. The 'set point' concept is supported by research that shows that people return to a characteristic level of happiness a short time after both unusually good and unusually bad events. But the research on gratitude suggests that people can move their 'set point' upward to some degree, enough to have a measurable effect on both their outlook and their health.

Summarizing the findings from studies to date, Emmons says that those who practice grateful thinking 'reap emotional, physical and interpersonal benefits'. People who regularly keep a gratitude journal report fewer illness symptoms, feel better about their lives as a whole, and are more optimistic about the future.

IV. Cut Loose

> *Some of us think holding on makes us strong, but sometimes it is letting go.*
>
> *– Herman Hesse*

I have found that each time I let something go, it pops up less and less frequently and it has less power over me.

♌

They laid him down in front of us. He was lifeless, but we were still hopeful, surrounding him, crying hysterically, but hopeful that he would get up. But he didn't. Rohit, my only brother, was two years younger to me and was the best-looking man in the family. He, his wife and their son were settling down in life. But destiny had another plan.

On that fateful day, while getting ready for his office, he had severe abdominal pain and was forced to consult a doctor. Never in my weirdest dream had I thought that it would turn out to be so serious. After a long and painful series of investigations and surgeries, he was diagnosed with cancer of the kidney, at the age of only thirty-three.

We all were completely shattered. It was the most difficult phase of our life and we tried our best to save him by all means. But as destiny has its own path, we couldn't save him. The last days of his life were so painful that at one stage, I could not see him in that condition and prayed to god to rid him of his pains. After that, he became almost unconscious and hardly survived for two days. It seemed that all his pains were gone; god had listened to my prayers.

He died in front of us. As a doctor, as a sister and as a human being, I couldn't do anything. He had gone on a new journey, all alone. And what did we do? We could do nothing. We just allowed him to go peacefully.

After he left us, everything changed. We changed; the people around us changed too. It was a new world for us, where death can come so easily, so untimely.

Time passed. We all moved on with life. Though our lives are full of emptiness, we've learned to deal with it. We've learned to smile in despair, to talk in silence and to live with death around us.

Though he is always there in our hearts and living without him is still painful, but I am peaceful that he is not in pain any more. *We let him go just to make sure that his pain and suffering were eliminated.*

Sometimes in life, despite all our efforts, it seems that nothing is working the way we want. It doesn't mean that our efforts were not enough or our plans were wrong. It simply means that whatever we want isn't meant for us, at least not for now.

In other words, you have to let things go at times. No matter how much you like a person, a job, a relationship... you have to let it go.

Though it may be disheartening to lose your loved ones, but in reality, it leaves a positive impact on you.

How?

It simply occurs by the theory of 'Releasing Yourself', i.e. after getting yourself free from the bond you realize that it was meant to be like this all along and your craving for that particular thing will ultimately decrease. I know that it may be very difficult to accept this, but this is how our mind works. And many times I've seen that *fear of the unforeseen is much more disturbing than the event itself.* Maybe we are trained in such a way that when any misfortune occurs, we cannot do anything because it has already happened by that time. So whether you like it or not, you have to bear it.

We must realize that nothing is permanent in this world. The more you cling onto something, the more stressful you will become. When you try to release yourself from that bond, stress will be present initially, but later it will gradually disappear.

The same way, some people in our life come for a limited time period and they have to leave us. No matter how much we may try to hold them back with us, we have to eventually let them go. The point here is to realize when to let go and when to hold back.

So, now you have to decide to let certain things from your life go. That unpleasant job, that arrogant partner who always puts himself / herself first, that black dress gifted by your friend that you couldn't wear because it was too short, that old sofa which has served its purpose now, and so on.

Whatever it is, I personally feel that one should try to make the parting a memorable event. The experience, the feelings which you have at that particular moment, can either make you a complete person or break you into pieces. So remember that sometimes the best thing to do is to let go peacefully and move on with life. It may be extremely painful for some close relations, but you have to bear the loss for the sake of your loved ones. You have to understand that it is the will of god and we all are helpless in such scenarios and to avoid the pain, the best thing to do is to learn to flow with god's will.

Now, this is another aspect of this plan, 'to flow with life'. Here I don't mean that you should stop trying or thinking about changing your life. I simply mean that if your efforts go in vain or they start hurting you, then you should stop all your efforts and instead prepare yourself to flow with the life which may turn towards some other direction. But most of the time, it is for your benefit only, whether you like it or not. The only thing we have to do is keep our faith intact.

I met this young lady at a recent event. She was a beautiful woman in her forties. I found her very attractive and thought that her husband must be madly in love with her. Later, I came to know that she was a successful entrepreneur and lived in the vicinity. She had lost her husband two years back while he was driving back from a party. I also learned that her husband was a womanizer and had many relationships outside their marriage. It was a shocking revelation for me that even such a nice and independent woman couldn't get a nice and loving husband. More than that, what troubled me was why had she tolerated all of it throughout her married life? She could have filed for a divorce in her early years, but she hadn't. She was trying to save her marriage and I must say that she did succeed in a way. But she failed to understand that they were not made for each other. They had to get separated anyhow, and it happened with the demise of her husband.

By any means, I'm not defending her husband here, but I simply want to convey that *sometimes in our life we have to lose our most loving thing just to protect ourselves or the other one.* We should realize that the thing or person is not meant for us and it has to go, so it's always better to give up on it. But as you know, it's not that easy. A lot of courage, maturity and faith in the name of god are required.

So here I want to describe a few points which may help you to let go and move with the flow of life:

1. Identify the areas of your life where you are facing continuous hurdles / problems. For instance, it may be a relationship, a job, a person, a gadget, a house, etc.
2. Try to assess the problem in detail. Here you can take the help of your close friends too, if you need to do so.
3. After pinpointing the problem, try to find out the solutions.

4. According to the 'rule of 3', make lists of at least three solutions to each problem.
5. Apply the solutions one by one. Here you can take the help of your friends again.
6. Ideally, by now, your problem should get solved.
7. If they still persist, then ask yourself, do you really want the particular thing / person in your life?
8. If yes, then try to find out more solutions or try again with the old ones.
9. If the problem is solved now, then consider yourself lucky, very lucky.
10. If not, then prepare yourself to live without that thing/ person and let it go.

At this point, you should understand that these things/ persons are not meant for you and you should let them go. Even if you get them at some points of your life, you'll lose them. So it's better to let them go and move on with the flow of life.

♌

B. How to Streamline your Life

I. Where One is Heading

> *We will either find a way, or make one.*
> *– Hannibal*

If you don't have a plan for your life, someone else does.

This is the first step to start the second phase of this plan. *Have a plan* for your life as you do with your child. This way it will become easier to manage and you'll feel more organized. Though it's true that every time, your life can't go according to your plan, but still try to follow what you have planned for it.

There are few dos and don'ts while planning your life:

1. Keep your passion, focus, interests, available resources, etc., under consideration.
2. Never compare your life with others, since they may follow another path.
3. Choose the plan which makes you happy after reaching the destination as well as throughout the journey itself.
4. Even after being cautious, still you may feel that this was not what you wanted to achieve. In that case, change the plan and take another path.
5. Very often, others may try to pull you down or distract you from your goal. Be focused and strong enough to not hear them.
6. But at the same time, be wise enough to take the advice of those who are your true well-wishers.
7. While planning, be prudent enough to make goals which are practically possible to achieve.
8. Don't be too rigid and never push yourself too hard.
9. Reward yourself for every achievement, however small it may be.
10. Life's unforeseen turns are important to keep in mind and be calm and patient while dealing with them.

These are a few basic points you have to keep in mind while planning your goal. Be it life or your child, it's not easy to decide which path will be best.

But at the same time, over thinking about it will not help, and that is the time when you should follow your gut feeling. Many times god wants to show us the best path for us and gives hints too. It's our duty to recognize those hints and choose the path which he has already created for us.

The other important thing is how to choose various paths for various categories of life. This is quite simple and you can divide it in as many categories as you want. A few examples are given to help you understand:

a. Personal development, including academic development and grooming.
b. Maintaining relationships
c. Professional excellence/ career options including primary, secondary, tertiary career, etc.
d. Home management
e. Stress management
f. Managing vacations/ entertainment
g. Managing hobbies, and so on...

The list can be endless, but I will focus on explaining a few examples mentioned above.

Personal development – Well, this is quite important and a vast topic to begin with and one can write a complete book about it. But here we will just discuss key points for making a goal for your personal development.

The first and foremost important point here is to understand that *you* are the core in this plan and everything rotates around you. So it is your responsibility to make yourself eligible for the chosen path.

Do whatever you can do to develop your overall personality. It can be your academic development, grooming of your appearance, to learn a hobby or a new language; anything which you think is important to enhance your confidence, should be done with great élan and as top priority.

Maintaining relationships – The relations in your life can be broadly divided into two groups which can further be divided into subtypes according to the priority and their place in your life-

Family – can be further divided into kids, spouse, parents, siblings, relatives, etc.

Friends – can also be divided into best friends, good friends, etc.

And according to these subtypes, you can easily maintain these people in your life as you know at what time and how you are supposed to deal with them.

Professional excellence – This is the arena which you would say is important and at the same time difficult to deal with. You meet various people; some may create the core of your team and make your life either very easy or they can make your life a living hell. In both these cases, you are not losing, but learning something. Sometimes it may also happen that you want to change as a person or you may have already changed just to deal with such difficult people. But in all these cases, you should remember that while it's okay to change yourself just to deal with these kind of people, it's not prudent to compromise with your morals and core values. It is always advisable to keep your values and morals above all these difficult personalities.

When I was teaching in a college, one of my subordinates was too competitive and really difficult to handle. She used to do all the things in her own favour with such cleverness that I never doubted her integrity and her loyalty towards me. But when I started realizing that she was not that simple and literally making my life hell, I started confronting her. My single aim was to indicate to her that I have totally understood her intentions and I was not going to be fooled by her any more. Though it was not easy to deal with her after that and things had become worse, but to maintain my integrity and self worth, it was a necessary action to be taken. Eventually, our equation changed completely. We were no longer friends, and we didn't share our day to day life with each other. But we were at peace. At least I was.

So if you have to decide to change yourself to deal with someone, change your attitude only. And believe me, most of the time, that's enough.

You can also think about your career options here, like primary or main career along with secondary and tertiary career. I know I may sound weird, but in my view, we should have at least three career options in our hand. And nurture at least your second career too besides the primary one, which may be your hobby, passion, etc., while you are still young. This is an important step to remain busy and stress free in your life.

Home management – The other day I was reading *Don't sweat the Small Stuff* by Richard Carlson and I understood why it was a best seller. Every page of this book will give you something to learn from. When it comes to home management, there may be at least a thousands points which you can use from this book. Because before managing a home, you have to learn to manage yourself and this book will tell you how.

As I said, before managing your home, you have to organize yourself, so take out a few minutes daily to make a to-do list for that day. Or better, for the next day too. In this way, it's easier to manage yourself, your home, kids, in fact, your whole life.

Stress management – Well, if I say that this is perhaps the most important part to manage in life, then I won't be wrong. You will completely agree with me, won't you? In the roller coaster ride of life, we need something or someone that can cushion our ride by any means. We need people for that, we need money, time, anything which can make things easier for us, now and in future too. Of course, it's not easy. Had it been easy, not so many people would have been stressful in the world.

So what is that one strategy which is helpful to de-stress you? In my view, that one strategy is 'willingness'. It's our willingness to move ahead, to ignore things and to come out of a situation. Again, I would say it's not easy. So what is the technique to stay away from stress?

Here you go:

1. As I described earlier, willingness to come out is the most important factor.
2. You have to commit to yourself that you will get out of it. The sooner, the better.
3. Once you decide that you don't want any more stress, shift your thoughts from the negative to the positive

ones. For example, if you have kids, think about them; your spouse, lover, your new house, new car, a new dress, or a new haircut. Think about anything which can give you happiness.

4. While shifting your thoughts towards positive ones, focus on them completely.

5. If in between, stressful negative thoughts surface, push them out and replace them with the positive ones.

6. Be grateful while focusing on the positive thoughts. Thank god and all the people who are the reason behind your smile.

7. Remind yourself often in the day that those negative thoughts are not worth your attention and you have more important and worthy things in your life.

8. Smile. That's it. As many times as you can.

9. Last but not the least, *give yourself time.* Even a small stressful incident may seem big in an acute phase and acute phase reactions are the most damaging to our lives.

10. So give yourself time and when that acute phase will be over, you will naturally feel better and stress free.

Managing vacations/ entertainment – This is indeed an integral part of stress management and if you manage it efficiently, then de-stressing can become fun.

Some ideas for this plan –

1. Keep aside one day every week for any outdoor activity and it can be anything, like watching a movie, visiting a mall, a park, a picnic spot or visiting your parents, old friend, siblings, or one's in-laws.

2. Similarly, keep aside one day of every week for a heart to heart talk with your loved ones.

3. Have an appointment in a health care center and a spa at least once every month or in two months.

4. Meet your inner self daily for at least ten minutes and have a detailed introspection every week.

5. Have at least one or two creative hobbies and nurture them.

6. 'An empty mind is a devil's workshop', so keep yourself busy by any constructive measure.

7. Make many small goals and set deadlines for them.

8. Reward yourself if you achieve the goal.

9. Make sure to go for a vacation twice in a year.

10. Choose calm and peaceful places for rejuvenation, like hills and beaches, and try to not go at the peak time so that you can relax sans the crowds.

II. Turn the Tides

> *The most successful people are those who are good at plan B.*
>
> *– James Yokke*

Well, this is what I would consider the most helpful part of living and that is *to have an alternate plan or plan B in your hands.* Of course you can't have an alternate plan for all of life's decisions, but you can surely have for quite a few.

In any stressful condition, the moment you think about the alternate plan, you immediately feel relaxed. Just try it once and you'll understand what I mean.

During our early married life, while struggling to have kids, I had many miscarriages, and at one point it seemed really difficult to complete those nine months without any hurdle. That is the time when I used this strategy and thought that I would adopt a baby if I couldn't conceive. You may think that what is new there? Every couple who can't have kids, thinks in the same way. I agree.

The only point here is *'to give equal weightage and importance to your alternate plan'*. If you have to adopt a child, then do it whole-heartedly. Any regret or any feeling of compromise should be avoided. There are several couples who can't even afford to adopt. So be grateful for every opportunity god has created for you.

I met this guy while going to my office. He was reading a book in a park. After that, I used to see him sitting and reading there every day. One day I went to him and asked about his life. What he told me in a nutshell was that he was an orphan living in an orphanage. He loved reading, so he went to a local school there and after that he completed his graduation from a university. Now he wanted to get a job and had applied for it. He also knew that he may or may not be selected for the job. So he had another plan. Till his result came out, he decided to read all the bestsellers. Wow, so interesting! Then I asked what was his plan and what did he gain from all these books? Experience, he replied. Experience for what? To become an author some day, he said, and I was spellbound. In fact, he was very clear about it. He had applied for the job. If he got it, good, but if he didn't, he would become an author. And that is what I mean by an alternate plan.

Now can you see how that guy was using his time and brain for an alternate career in advance? The same way, we can use this plan for different challenges and problems in our life. Every problem has more than one solution. So what you have to do is to have at least three solutions in your hand for a single problem.

And what should be the strategy while applying your thoughts to alternate paths?

Here are the tricks:

1. Any problem, situation should be assessed deeply in all the areas.
2. While assessing your life, keep in mind to be fair with it.
3. Try to divide your life into various parts.
4. Find three ('Rule of 3') ways to deal with all aspects of your life – personal, professional, etc.
5. Never ever consider an alternate path to be a secondary one, but give it equal importance.
6. Believe in your decisions fully.
7. Don't listen to others' views about your life because it's your life and you are the best judge of it.
8. Make sure that your alternate chosen path is easier or at par with the main path, only then you can be sure enough to follow it.
9. When choosing the alternate path, make it a point that it should give you almost the same happiness and feeling of worth as you'll get from the main path.
10. Now, just go for it!

There are few examples which tell you how to use this exercise in day to day life and the simple rule is 'rule of 3', which says to make a list of the best three of each:

1. Schools
2. Houses
3. Society
4. Dresses
5. Furniture
6. Colleges
7. Careers
8. Job opportunities
9. Even friends
10. Your family physicians
11. Nearby hospitals
12. IVF centers
13. Grocery vendors
14. TV shows
15. Daily meals
16. Weekend outings
17. Office spaces
18. Colleagues
19. Ways of working
20. Solutions to the problems
21. Social services
22. Car models

And the list goes on. The idea here is to shrink all the possibilities to the best three and consider them as important as the main one.

This way you will have three options in your hand and it definitely increases your chances of getting at least one out of the three possibilities.

Obviously, when there are more choices, there are better chances to get at least one choice. So stick to minimum three alternate choices to ease your life and to make it stress free.

So now onwards, make it a habit to instantly think about all the alternate solutions of any problem. Think about them deeply and own all of them as a possible outcome of that problem. Give them equal importance to make you stress free and calm in all situations. The more you practice this, the more you will be able to handle the pressure from any stream of life.

III. The Ways and Means

> *Money only goes where we tell it to go, so know where you are sending it.*
> *At the end 'Sense of Money' matters.*

Well, in simpler form, get employed to have enough money to live comfortably.

In fact, this is the topic which should be taken at the very beginning of this book as it is one of the most important parts of living. The reason I took it up midway is because you should think about it immediately after closing this book.

In today's world, it is very disheartening to see that people measure your success with your net worth. I differ a little bit and consider satisfaction and contentment as bigger tools to measure one's success. But it cannot be denied that money plays a very important part in our lives. A lot of problems and worries can be minimized if you are financially strong. At the same time, you need to earn for your livelihood.

In my view, every person on this earth should be independent enough to deal with one's normal life, financially, physically, mentally and emotionally. For that you need life skills so you should learn to earn, to cook, to wash; in fact, to do all sorts of work required to live comfortably.

So when you decide to earn, you have to think about a career. And when you think about a career, I'll advise you to choose it wisely. The basic rule of thumb is to choose a career in the field of your passion. No matter how silly it may seem initially, but if you love something and want to pursue it your whole life, then go ahead. You can only succeed in your career if you really love your work.

So how can you choose your area of work? Here are a few guidelines to begin with. You can see the chapter titled 'Follow Your Passion' later for more details.

1. Try to recall what you loved to do most during your childhood days.
2. Can you make it your career?
3. If no, then can you make your career in other similar fields?
4. If no, then why? Do you require learning some skills?
5. If yes, then start taking lessons in it.
6. Remember, there is no age bar for your passion.
7. You can excel in anything if you focus on it completely for three years.
8. When it comes to your dreams, three years of your life (from life expectancy of approximately 60-80 years) are not a big deal, are they?
9. In fact, this is an investment and it is always better to invest in something you like to do rather than to waste your whole life doing something you never loved.
10. So take a deep breath and start today!

Fine, so now you have made a decision about your career and I'm pretty sure that you will do great in it and will emerge out as a successful person.

Here, I remember a story of an artist whose passion was singing. He chose music as his career and was earning well through his stage performances and music classes. He was doing fine and living comfortably with his wife and a son. But somewhere in the line, he was lacking that 'sense of money'. So you want to know, what is the 'sense of money'?

Let me tell you that it is no different from 'sense of humour' or 'sense of music'. A 'sense of money' is your ability to deal well with your money. And I have seen many people lacking this sense and thus not utilizing their money properly and effectively, resulting in a stressful life. The same happened with this fellow. Somehow at the end of the month, he was always short of money to pay the bills.

I suggested that there were two options to deal with it: either they (he and his wife) should work as a unit or they should work as two different units. Though it is always better to work as a unit, but believe me, most of the time it is the most difficult task to do so even in the happiest of families. And I always prefer that spouses should act as two units and should divide their work areas so that there are fewer differences to tackle.

Further, I recommend a few good reads like *Secrets of the Millionaire Mind* by T. Harv Eker or 'The Truth About Money' by Rick Edelman, and other similar books which can help you to learn everything about your finances.

However, one thing that you should always remember is to give money a place in your pocket only and not in the heart. Money should give you a comfortable life and not a competitive and stressful one.

Many times, money may become a major cause of clashes between relatives, friends and even between the spouses.

For spouses, here are a few words of wisdom. They should understand that the partners are from different families; their upbringing is different and so is their way of dealing with money, or you can say 'sense of money'. Whatever may be the case, stinginess and over-expenditure should be avoided. And you should also remember that money is a form of energy, and to maintain its regular flow, you need to spend your money too. In fact, saving and spending money should go side by side. And you know that if you do it wisely, money can become a lifelong partner which can support you through the hardships of life.

IV. Create Space for New Happenings

Collect moments, not things.

You can never be happy, nor can you live your life fully, if you are surrounded by clutter.

This message says it all. You have to create space for new thoughts, new happiness, new ideas, etc., and that cannot be done until you get rid of surrounding clutter. Clutter here doesn't mean only physical objects, but emotional or mental too, and this particularly happens when we are too involved with a lot of things.

To live a happy and fulfilled life, clarity of thoughts is an essential requirement. You should think rationally about any issue or problem in your life. And you can't do that if your mind is already occupied with too many thoughts. When we have minimum things or thoughts around us, or you can say when we have minimum clutter surrounding us, we have less worries and liabilities which equates to less stress. And when we have less stress and worries, we will have more satisfaction and contentment in our life.

So it is a good idea to delete all the clutter surrounding you which may be physical (includes clothes, books, toys, etc.), emotional (includes grudges, negative thoughts, jealousy, anger etc.) and in today's scenario, digital (addictive gadgets) as well.

So, the best thing to do is to set a limit for 'amount and time' and this rule is known as the 'rule of 3' again. And this rule says that you can stick to any three issues or ideas or thoughts for three days only.

So what are you supposed to do here? First we'll delete our mental clutter by this method:

1. Select any three thoughts/ ideas/ issues which are disturbing you the most and you want to deal with them first.
2. Arrange them in an order according to their priority.
3. Give yourself a time limit of three days to deal with them.
4. Make sure you do everything you can to deal with them.
5. In between, if any new problem arises, then you have to delete one. So first deal with the one which is the easiest to solve and delete it to create space for the new one.
6. This way, you have to keep maximum three problems in your mind at a given time.
7. The moment you realize that the number is increasing, you have to deal with one and solve it before deleting it from your mind.

8. Sometimes, there may be issues which cannot be solved in the three day time period. In that case, you can keep that issue for more than three days but solve the remaining ones.

9. The idea is to keep only three issues at a time and stick to it.

10. If you are still burdened with more than three issues, then try to pass on one issue to someone else in the form of a responsibility so that it can be solved and at the same time you can stick to the 'rule of 3'.

11. Remember, 'no. 3' is the maximum limit for the amount as well as for the days, so try to solve the issues before that, better if you can do that on day one itself!

Now, if I tell you about how to remove your physical clutter then I'm pretty sure that most of you will be having much better ideas than me. Moreover, this can never be told in a few pages; a whole book will be needed for that.

So I won't go in much detail, but would just tell you the easiest way to remove physical clutter. The best thing you can do is to apply a minimalistic approach to everything. And few ideas can be taken from here:

1. You can buy fewer clothes and reuse them after washing and ironing.

2. The books which you have already read can be donated to a library. Though as a voracious reader, I always suggest to have a small and good library in the house which should include all the classics and bestsellers so that you can read a book any time. That way you

are never alone and can always enjoy the company of books.

3. You can pool toys and books for your kids.

4. Minimum furniture in the house gives a lot of space and also keeps your mind in sync with the ambience.

5. The same way, gadgets should be fewer in number and should suffice the basic usage only. The more advanced the technology, the more your mind will be occupied. And when you are occupied mentally, you can never feel calm and peaceful.

6. Work on the theory of 'demand and supply' and buy only those things that you really need.

7. Lastly, keep your needs minimum, so that no clutter ever accumulates in your house.

8. When you have no clutter in your house, your efficiency to do things will improve too.

9. When you efficiently do the things and finish your tasks completely, you will feel happy and fulfilled right from your inner self.

10. And this happiness and fulfillment is the key towards a fulfilling life.

V. The Unwritten laws

The unwritten laws here imply that there should be few rituals in your life which you should practice on daily basis. These rituals are very easy to perform, but definitely need your thought shift, consistency and perseverance.

a. Keep it Simple

Simplicity is the ultimate sophistication.
– Leonardo da Vinci

This is a known fact that the simpler is our life, the merrier we are. But still, knowingly or unknowingly, we make our lives so complicated that it becomes difficult to deal with. Now just imagine a newborn baby. He is so simple and innocent that we instantly fall in love with him. A grown up kid who is not simple but street smart, instantly puts us off. Isn't it true? It is because we love simplicity in everything.

But what is a simple life?

A simple life is one where you remain happy and content with whatever you have. You have no grudges and you love yourself and your life just the way you love your child. It's that simple.

If we like everything simple, then why shouldn't our lives be free of all complexities too? It is true that with so much shrewdness around it may not be possible to remain simple throughout your life. At a certain point you may realize that someone is using you or taking advantage of your innocence. To this I can only say that we should keep our eyes open and accept this fact that many people we meet in our lives are not the way we expect them to be. They may be shrewd, competitive and jealous, but these are the people who make our lives complete. Life is a journey which includes good as well as bad experiences and we can't expect everything to be hunky dory. There are people who will be difficult to read or analyze and this is the bitter truth.

I won't say that everyone is like that, but some of them are definitely like that and you have to bear with them. A harsh truth of the society is that people seek to have comparisons with everyone in the minutest details. And unfortunately, you can't change their mindset.

But yes, you can certainly do something about it just to protect yourself from becoming a person like them. And that is what I mean by simplicity here.

The basic thing you can do here is to choose your friends wisely because *you become what your friends are*. An old friend who has grown up with you is the best bet and has greater trust factor than a new one. They are much better choices to share your excitement or dilemmas with.

If you are not fortunate enough to have an old friend or a reliable one, then you need to trust your parents, siblings or partner, and yes, your kids too.

The only thing I want to convey here that despite the types of people you get to meet in your life, you should stick to your core values. And that is the simplest way to lead a simple life.

And when you want to live a simple life, you need to accept the faults and mistakes of the people and still believe in their goodness. And that is the true simplicity of a person.

So what are the strategies that can help you maintain the simplicity of your life?

1. Always try to stick to your core values.
2. Do what you consider is right in particular circumstances, irrespective of others' views.
3. Always keep your conscience alive and listen to your inner voice.
4. Do everything for the right reasons and things will fall into place.

5. Never compare your life with others' and that is one of the best solutions to remain happy and content.
6. Stick to your roots. I got this valuable advice from my mom-in-law, that one of the easiest ways to stick to your roots is to keep in touch with your near and dear ones.
7. Call them often and talk about the good old days, the memories of which can delight you.
8. Better still is to meet them often.
9. So assign one day of every week for a talk over phone and assign one day every month or two to meet them.
10. Being in touch with your near and dear ones keeps you grounded and that is the first requirement to lead a simple life.

The key is to be a simple and lovable person, but at the same time, be wise enough to mark a difference between the genuine and fake gestures of a person. And then act accordingly. Be simple, not foolish!

b. Don't Cry Over Spilled Milk

Happiness comes when we stop complaining about the troubles we have and offer thanks for all the troubles we don't have.

Yes, you should never complain about the miseries of life. Life goes on with all its positive and negative aspects. When we complain about something, we actually focus on that; anything on which we focus or concentrate tends to expand. In other words, the more you complain, the further your problems will expand. So make it a point to not to concentrate on your problems, rather concentrate on your blessings.

Again, I would say it's not easy and a lot of courage is needed. Here are a few points which you can keep in mind while dealing with this problem of complaining:

1. While thinking of complaining, just check yourself then and there, before you even say it aloud.
2. Always have this habit of rehearsing your thoughts before you speak. This way you can check any unnecessary words or complaints coming out of your mouth.
3. If you failed to check it and said something already, then just bite your tongue as soon as you realize and never linger on it.
4. At the same time, promise yourself not to do it again.
5. Try to analyze every complaint you are about to say, or even if you have said it, because we human beings have unnecessary issues with almost everything.
6. This habit of us makes our life miserable if we don't train our brain to see positivity in every situation.
7. We should realize that everything happens for a reason and whether we like it or not, these are necessary parts of our life which shape us as a human being.
8. Moreover, crying every time over trivial issues make us more tense and stressful.
9. Also by doing so we come across as an inefficient person because of our incapability to handle the situation.
10. So the best bet is to keep these small day to day worries to yourself, solve them efficiently and prove that you can, at least to yourself, if not to others.

I have seen many people who have limitations in life in any form – financial, physical and emotional. But they chose not to complain and to be happy with whatever little they had in their hands. And that is the key to a fulfilling life because we can never be happy if we are always seeing what we don't have rather than what we have.

I still remember how my mother used to make a budget for her monthly expenditures. The month in which she complained about extra expenses, for some reason or another, she had to spend more than the allocated amount. Thus, her monthly budget used to get completely shattered. I then advised her not to complain about this and she stopped this habit of complaining. Now her finances are pretty much in her control.

So never complain, instead be grateful for what you have, even if you think that it is much less. Because somewhere someone is struggling to get even that much. If you are leading a comfortable life and if you can afford basic needs of life, then I don't think that you have any reason to complain.

One of the most common reasons to gripe is to compare our lives with others and that is the main reason of our unhappiness. We can't digest this fact that someone is doing better than us, and knowingly or unknowingly, we start finding those areas where that person is lagging behind. And that gives us instant pleasure.

As a human being we want to show our greatness or that we are best or above all others. I won't say that if you think so, then you are wrong; absolutely not. But if you want to prove your greatness by putting others down, then it's not right. You can be a great human being only if you uplift yourself as well as others so that all of them can accept the fact that you are actually superior to them and that will be your true victory. So start uplifting yourself and others, rather than putting someone down, and then only you can lead a blissful life.

c. The Three Inch Curve

> *Smile doesn't necessarily mean you are happy. Sometimes it just means you're strong.*

Happiness is something everyone strives for on a day-to-day basis, a sense of well-being which leaves you feeling accomplished and often fulfilled at the end of the day.

Every day I come across so many people, some of them are friends, some are not. But one thing is common between most of them: that they are not happy. I won't say that people are sad, but somehow they are not happy. Some of them have horrible mothers-in-law; some have control-freak husbands, and still others have difficult bosses. Some are lonely; others are living with a crowd. Some are not happy due to their spoilt kids; others have kids who are simpletons. Some are poor; others are rich, but still not happy. I mean to say here that due to some reason or another, people don't want to be happy.

Yes, they don't *want* to stay happy because they have designed their lives around others. A person will be happy if her spouse, mother-in-law, boss, kids, neighbours, etc., will lead their lives according to *her*. Seriously, we want everyone to work according to our expectations and any deviation from that is enough to make us tense, anxious and even sad.

So why can't we be happy on our own? Why should *our* happiness depend on *others*?

The answer lies within the question itself. The path to happiness is all our own. It's our life, our happiness, so we should learn to be happy. And how can we achieve it? The answer is simple: 'By having less expectations'. Whether it's your hubby, kids, parents, parents-in-law, colleagues or even *you* yourself, drop your expectations and you'll be a lot happier. Better still to have no expectations at all. I know it's difficult but not impossible.

Smile,
Smile, if you feel low;
Smile when you feel high.
Smile in despair;
Smile in love.
Smile, when you can;
Smile, when you can't.
Smile, when things go wrong;
Smile, when you find them right.
Smile, when everything you get;
Smile, when your eyes are wet.

So keep smiling in every circumstance, but sometimes you may find it difficult to smile even if you try very hard and that is when you need all the more reason to smile.

I'll tell you a very easy and sure shot way to make you smile often:

1. Sit calmly where you are right now.
2. Hold your breath for a few seconds.
3. Remove all thoughts from your mind.

4. Now try to remember any funny thing / incident / joke.
5. Instant smile appears on your face; hold it, acknowledge it.
6. Try to see yourself in a mirror, if feasible (in a car, washroom, etc.)
7. Appreciate yourself in the smiling portrait because you really look beautiful while smiling.
8. Try to remember your beautiful smiling face and fix it in your mind.
9. Try to remember it often, appreciate it and do smile again.
10. You may notice that others also acknowledge you more when you smile and this is reason enough to smile again *and* again.

If we look at it medically also, it is proven that the more we smile the more healing will occur. When we smile, a lot of our facial muscles get contracted and relaxed, which result in a lot of facial exercises.

A smile is one thing that can win you a lot of friends because we all like a person with a beautiful smile. And believe me, a smile is always beautiful. It gives you as well as others, instant warmth, calmness and happiness. It also makes you comfortable, enhances your faith in people and increases your desire to live again.

And I don't think that these are any less reasons to smile more.

A study from Pennsylvania State University found that people who smile appear to be more likeable, courteous and even more competent.

Researchers at Uppsala University in Sweden concluded that frowning when looking at someone smiling is possible, but would be very difficult.

When you smile, your brain is aware of the activity and actually keeps track of it. The more you smile, the more effective you are at breaking the brain's natural tendency to think negatively. If you smile often enough, you end up rewiring your brain to make positive patterns more often than the negative ones.

Shawn Achor dubs retraining our 'brain to scan for the good things in life – to help us see more possibility, to feel more energy, and to succeed at higher levels' as 'The Positive Tetris Effect' in his book *The Happiness Advantage*. His argument is that the popular game Tetris has a tendency to make such an impression on players that after it's been shut off, people still see Tetris blocks in real life. According to Achor, we can do the same thing by practicing a more positive thinking pattern, which ultimately creates a happiness loop.

Achor writes:

'Happiness is a work ethic… It's something that requires our brains to train just like an athlete has to train.'

The biochemist Sondra Barrett claims in her book *Secrets of Your Cells* that when you let go of tension – an outcome that can be achieved through smiling – your cells let go of their rigidness. According to Barrett's research, this could end up saving your life as there have been cases where cancer patients go into remission of cancer after letting go of a big stress factor.

In an article by Roger Dooley in *Forbes*, author writes that decades of research bear out the basic truth: your mood is elevated and your stress is reduced if you plaster a big smile on your face, even for a short period of time. (Frowns have been shown to have the opposite effect.) The smile doesn't have to be based on real emotion – faking it works.

d. Commune with God

> *"For I know the plans I have for you," declares the Lord,*
> *"plans to prosper you and not to harm you, plans to give*
> *you hope and a future." (Jeremiah 29:11)*

I agree with you if you say that to pray or not to pray is an individual's choice, but here, I mean to say that if you pray, things will become a lot more simple.

Why is it so?

It is simply because when you pray, you actually surrender yourself to the Almighty and you believe that now you are taken care of. That belief is all that we need to remain calm in any situation.

That is the reason I believe in the power of a prayer.

Pray often, or at least once in a day. *Pray not to please god; pray just to please yourself, to make yourself calm and peaceful.* And this can be done by thanking god enough for surplus blessings that he has bestowed upon you rather than asking anything from him.

Prayer evokes that strong feeling inside you which can create miracles in no time. Somewhere during my college days, I've read these two lines which I still believe completely.

It's faith in the name of the Lord, Which works wonders.

Those who have faith have everything, Faith is life, doubt is death.

If you believe in these lines, then I bet, you'll feel the amazing sense of security instantly and your worries and anxiety will go away.

I learned this the other day while talking to my father.

"God gives us strength in all crises, which is directly proportional to the crises itself."

That's all. So, stay positive and calm in every situation. Rest, god will take care of.

You know what is the best thing to do in times of such crises? To surrender to god or to your loved ones. It's an amazing feeling which completely relaxes our mind and our worries drift away.

Though there is one condition before surrendering and that condition is to have 'faith' in the name of god or in that person. Complete faith is required, without any doubt, to do wonders, because faith is life and doubt is death.

In fact, 'faith' is that amazing factor which gives us 'hope' in every situation. When we are hopeful, we remain 'positive' in all aspects of life, even in the worst of situations.

Really, parents are a great source of inspiration, aren't they?

Yes, they are, and when such advice comes from parents, it becomes much more authentic. So keep your faith alive, have a positive mindset and wait for the wonders to happen.

That day I received this beautiful video, where the lady in the video was explaining the right technique to pray. I want to summarize it here for you:

1. Just join both your hands in a 'namaste'.
2. Now concentrate on your hands and your fingers individually.
3. As you can see that your thumbs are closest to your heart, it denotes those people who are closest to you like family and friends, pray for them.

4. Your index finger is the one which you use to point out to others. Pray for them too.

5. Your middle finger is the tallest. It denotes all the people who have a higher place in your heart: your teachers, your ideals, etc., pray for them.

6. The ring finger is said to be the weakest link of your hand, denoting all the people who are weak or poor. Pray for them as they need it the most.

7. Now come to the last one and that is the little finger; it denotes you. You have already prayed for so many people that god himself will provide everything to you without you even asking for it.

Now can you see how wonderfully you can pray and that too in almost no time? You barely need five minutes to do this, but you can achieve a great sense of fulfillment in your life.

One more important point I need to add here is that while praying, never ask what you want; instead ask what is right for you. Because you can ask anything seeing your current situation only and later may regret your decision. So have faith in almighty as he can decide in a better way what is best for you.

The other great point about prayer is that you can talk to god if you want to and I'm not joking, it is true. Many authors and self help gurus have already written about it and I too have experienced this divine power many times.

Let me tell you the easiest technique to do that:

1. Choose a suitable time and a quiet place to pray.

2. Burn some incense for a calm ambience.

3. Take a rug or a mat on which you can sit comfortably. If you can't sit for long, then take some back support. Now sit comfortably on the mat.

4. Close your eyes and think about god, whom you have complete faith in.

5. Call him in front of you and imagine that he is sitting there. And believe me, he is sitting there.

6. Have a heart to heart conversation with him; better to say it aloud. Pour your heart out, cry, laugh, and say whatever you want to say. In other words, surrender yourself completely.

7. While talking, you can see the expressions of your god. Try to read those expressions.

8. Take as long as you need to complete the prayer. At last, pay gratitude with a smile on your face.

9. Open your eyes and look around. How do you feel? If you feel completely relaxed and calm, then your prayer is successful.

10. It needs practice, but eventually you will learn this technique and start feeling better day by day.

Author Clay Routledge wrote in an article in *Psychology Today* that recent research indicates that prayer can help you get more out of your 'self-control muscle'. Research participants who said a prayer prior to a mentally exhausting task were better able to exercise self-control following that task. In addition, other studies demonstrate that prayer reduces alcohol consumption, which may reflect the exercise of self-control. Findings such as these suggest that prayer has an energizing effect.

He further writes that researchers found that having people pray for those in need reduced the amount of aggression they expressed following an anger-inducing experience.

Researchers also found that people who prayed for others were less vulnerable to the negative physical health effects.

e. The Dark Glasses

> *The art of being wise is the art of knowing what to overlook.*
>
> –William James

This simply means overlooking the small things or mistakes of people. I know many of you may not agree, but it is *most certainly* the best policy for peace of mind. The main reason behind any disappointment is our detailed analysis and interpretation of a particular thing which can be anything – a talk, a comment, a compliment, an incidence and so on. To overcome this, the best idea is to not do a detailed analysis until it is asked for.

And believe me, it's a necessary action to maintain peace of your mind. I have seen many people who lose their sleep over other's opinions and comments which is not good for their overall well being. What others think or do is their personal matter and we should not entangle our lives with their thought processes.

So here are a few points which will help you to deal with such people/circumstances:

1. Ignore them, if doing so maintains the peace of your mind.
2. To overlook day to day small things should be a mandatory task of your daily routine

3. To accuse your spouse and to complain about his / her trivial mistakes are not wise things to do and it can eventually ruin your married life.

4. Never waste your energy and time to analyze a person, comment, opinion, or a situation in detail unless it is asked for.

5. Always give a person the benefit of doubt for the first mistake or maybe for two. Never ignore the third one and confront the person straightforward.

6. Ignorance is the best policy, unless you are taken for granted. And you should be wise enough to see the difference.

7. Remember that you are ignoring things for the peace of your mind. Don't expect the other person to change overnight or to apologize for their mistakes.

8. Don't put yourself in the list of great people because you have ignored a particular thing for your inner peace.

9. Be balanced and prudent enough to understand the need of the hour and act accordingly.

10. Sometimes it is a strict no to ignore something. Recognize those situations and then act.

Here, I remember one of my colleagues. She was otherwise happy and led a blissful life, but she had this irritating habit of dissecting each and everything said or done by others. She would go to the extremes of her thoughts in speculating and interpreting what others meant when they had said or done a particular thing. She would be having endless discussions with her near and dear ones, thus making her own and others' lives miserable. I told her many times to quit this habit, but in vain. Finally, I decided to teach her a lesson. I started dissecting her each and every word and started confronting her. She tried to explain herself initially, but later pleaded with me to not do this as she could not afford so much stress. Then I told her that this is what she had been doing to herself and others throughout her life. She understood immediately and promised to quit the habit. Needless to say, now she is happier and more peaceful in life. She has learnt the art to ignore and let go and not to hold on to the unnecessary things in life.

I have seen many spouses who look for a little mistake of their partners and then make a big mountain of it. They'll argue to prove themselves right and to belittle their partners.

What is the point?

No one in this world is perfect and we as humans are bound to make mistakes. In fact, these human errors are a big source of our learning. You forget to take your house key one day and the problems you faced due to that will never allow you to repeat that mistake again. The bigger the mistake, the more it will stick to your brain that you cannot afford that mistake again. It is that simple.

So next time when you notice a mistake, just overlook it, because every mistake holds a blessing with it. Moreover, you should also realize that that person is already suffering due to his / her mistake, so it's not humane to torture him / her again and again.

f. Be Where You Are – Mindfulness

Live in the moment and make it beautiful.

In other words, you can say that one should live in the present, and not only live, you should give your hundred percent attention to the work at hand. Yes, you have read it right.

Though we combine mindfulness with meditation but mindfulness is not necessarily about meditation only; it simply means to be aware of whatever you are doing. For example, if you are cooking, then full awareness of everything right from the chopping of vegetables, cooking them, and making the accompanying chapattis is needed. And that is mindfulness.

So you can see that it can be anything. An extremely important work or your daily routine; you have to do everything with full concentration.

And if you follow this, you'll get plenty of benefits and a few of which I'm listing here:

1. Any work if done with full awareness, concentration and focus tends to give you the best results.
2. Full concentration means that you are thinking about the work which is in your hands.
3. It also means that your brain is occupied by that work only and you have no space and no time to think about something else.
4. So you cannot think about anything beyond that means no worries and no negative thoughts.
5. If worries or negative thoughts are absent, then it means that you are content and happy.
6. So you can see this way that mindfulness can be a great tool to bring you happiness and satisfaction.
7. When you are happy and content, you can lead a fulfilled life and do all your tasks more efficiently.
8. When you give full attention to any work, you will remember it for long.

9. In other words, forgetfulness and carelessness will vanish and you'll come across as a more efficient and capable person.

10. So, it is recommended to follow mindfulness daily as a tool for a happy and fulfilled life.

When we talk about mindfulness, many things can be found out on the internet and in various books. But here I only want to elaborate the simple fact of awareness. To be there and focus in the present moment and nothing more.

So how can you practice mindfulness in day to day life? The internet is full of many techniques, most of which are associated with meditation. If you can follow them then, nothing like that.

But due to hectic and busy life schedules, many of us do not get enough time to set aside some time for meditation. In that case, we have to train our mind for 'mindfulness' simultaneously while doing our daily work. Isn't it a good idea? That way we can save time and can complete the assigned tasks too.

Following steps will teach you this technique:

1. Most important thing is to keep your eyes open. (Paradox here, as most of the literature will tell you to close your eyes.)

2. And now the more important thing is to connect your eyes with your mind. The technique to do it is to tell your mind continuously what you are doing. For instance, you can say 'I am washing carrots. Now I am peeling them with a peeler knife. Now I am cutting them. And so on'.

3. It's just like a 'demonstration of any project' where you want to tell your audience about anything in detail to

make them aware of whatever you are doing. Here your audience is your 'mind'. This is a conscious process and it will come naturally with practice.

4. Now, to master this, you have to train your mind again and again.
5. Your eyes move faster than your mind so you have to push your mind where your eyes move.
6. Your mind will try to distract you many times. Don't listen to it.
7. Continuously guide your mind where it has to go.
8. However, sometimes your eyes too wander, and in that case, you have to stick to the work you are doing.
9. When there is any confusion or disagreement, stop that work then and there.
10. The best option in that scenario is to take a break, like a quick nap. You'll feel much better after the rest and can continue your work.

This way, you can train your mind to be aware of everything you are doing. Initially it may be a little difficult, but soon you will get used to it.

C. How to fulfill your life's Dream

I. Discipline your Life

> *The distance between dreams and reality is called discipline.*

Well, this is the first and most important step towards making your dreams come true. You have to discipline your life the way you discipline your child. And why do you do that with your child? It is simply because you want him or her to be successful in life. You want your child to achieve something big so that you can be proud of your child, right?

So, if you think so much about your child, then why not about your life? By inculcating discipline in your life you can also achieve something big. So be a disciplined person and live your life in a way that it can set an example for others.

And when we talk about discipline, then we should learn it from sportpersons. Most of them are very particular about their daily routine and tasks. They plan their all activities on a daily basis. They do exercises and yoga to make their life more focused and fulfilled.

Though I agree that discipline is not merely about exercise or yoga, but it includes a life taken well with all its ups and downs.

A disciplined life actually means a 'structured life' which simply means a life which is to be lived properly, despite its not so proper ways. I mean to say here that you have to survive with dignity through all the ups and downs of life.

And I know it's not easy. In fact, to live a disciplined life is one of the most difficult tasks because we all sometimes in our lives are forced to surrender to the temptations the world gives us. Not do so is what I believe comprises discipline.

So, to have a structured or disciplined life, you need certain ingredients, and they are:

1. Integrity
2. Passion
3. Focus
4. Punctuality

5. Compassion
6. Sincerity
7. Efficiency
8. Competence
9. Hard work
10. Self control

If you ask me, then I personally feel that the first and last are the main ingredients for a disciplined life. Though it is also true that both go hand in hand; you need integrity to keep your conscious alive, while self control is needed to avoid all the temptations or distractions, and this is the first thing to help you towards your dreams.

So how can you lead a disciplined life to fulfill your dreams? I'm going to tell you the easiest way:

1. Make a life plan according to your dream / passion.
2. Don't include anything which distracts you from your goal.
3. See how feasible this plan is and how much work it needs.
4. Remove all unrealistic goals from the list.
5. Now, make a list of all the things you need to follow that plan and apply them.
6. Are you happy with the results?
7. If yes, then go ahead with the plan.
8. If not, then ask yourself why it is so. Try to find out the reason.
9. Reconsider and re-apply the plan.
10. Make yourself free to activate this plan so that you can achieve whatever you want from life.

You can see here that just like you have to discipline your child, you also have to discipline your life in a way that it can take the shape of your desired life. Compassion, strictness, hard work and other essential points mentioned above are the key points to make your dreams come true.

It is only you who will determine and bring your life to the right track. And what is the right track for your life? It's the path of your dreams and passion. The more you'll be focused on the right track, the smoother and more fulfilling your life journey will be.

So keep moving on the right track and enjoy the journey.

II. A 180 Degree turn

The only criterion to bounce back is to touch the bottom.

Many times in life we find ourselves standing at a point from where many roads can take you to different destinations. Choosing the right track becomes extremely difficult. Even if you take a thoughtful decision, it may either lead to a fulfilled and happy life or a miserable life that is full of complexities. It doesn't matter how hard you try, but sometimes, you find yourself at a blind end from where you find no way to move further.

In such a scenario, when nothing works, you should take a 180 degree turn, touch rock bottom and bounce back again.

Bring everything to zero and then start again from scratch. Many times, our past holds us so strongly that even if we are doing our best, we are going nowhere. The main reason for which is the entanglement we face in our life and this entanglement is the result of our decisions which sometimes go awfully wrong. And as with all other human beings, we too hesitate to accept that we have taken some wrong steps. That denial to accept our mistakes results in a life that is miserable. And surely, none of us want to live such a life.

In such a scenario, it is always better to turn your life 180 degrees. But before you take this step, you have to accept that your past was not perfect and that is the reason that you need to start from scratch. That realization to begin your life again may be a little disheartening because you have to change everything to come out from that comfort zone. Again, I would say it's not easy but you have to do it, because you are not left with any other choice.

When you think of doing so, you may have two doors open in front of you:

1. One is easier to follow and that demands just to change one part / field of your life, for example, your career / job. Though the part you are going to change is really important and eventful for your life, but as a major portion of your life remains the same – like family, friends, and your native place – it is still easier to make this change.

2. The other path is somewhat difficult as it is done in extreme cases – a point when you may have hit rock bottom and from there it is not easy to start or rise again. But as I said earlier too, it may not be easy initially, but later you'll realize a great sense of self worth and authority over your own life.

I remember two such incidents, where both of them took a turn and began living their life on their own terms.

Riya was my colleague and at a very young age of thirty-three, she lost her husband in an accident. She didn't have any child to look after either. So she decided to start life all over again. She was very clear that she wanted peace of mind and didn't want to get involved in any legal hassle with her in-laws.

So she decided to set her in-laws free, as they wanted to cut all ties with her and move on. Without giving it a second thought, she moved in with her parents, closed all the legal issues with her in-laws and continued with her job to survive. In my view, her decision to leave everything she shared with her husband for her in-laws, may not be practically right, but it was correct if we take into consideration her mental status. Having done so, she is now at peace because she is far away from the judgmental eyes of everyone, including her in-laws. And for whatever she did, I admire her courage and selflessness.

The major factor for her survival might be her professional stability. She was employed in a good institute and earning a decent amount. I know that a complete turn is difficult for a person who is financially not strong, and in those cases, other ways should be sought.

Then there is one of my close friends, who also lost her husband at the age of thirty-five. Within no time she decided to move away from the place. She, along with her seven-year-old daughter moved to Bangalore from Delhi. It was a completely new place for her, but she quit her job and moved to start her life afresh. Now she is happy and bringing up her daughter very well. And I must say that this is the real 180 degree turn and I'm really proud of her.

Now you can understand what I meant by a 180 degree turn to your life. I agree that by doing so, you may have to lose a lot, but remember, the amount of happiness and self worth you get by doing so will be far more precious than your financial loss.

So how and why can a 180 degree turn in your life be helpful?

1. Sometimes it may be the only way to protect your dignity and self respect.
2. You have touched rock bottom and starting again from scratch which is enough to weigh your worth in your own eyes.
3. One thing should be remembered – it is always prudent to turn your life on a path that is known to you.
4. If you are clueless about the path, then don't take the turn, instead learn about something you want to do first, and then take the risk.
5. Initially, it may be difficult to cope up with the new world as any change from the routine always brings a certain amount of anxiety and depression.
6. Give yourself time. As you know that you have nothing else to look upon, try to get motivation from the smallest achievements.
7. When you start from zero, chances to take risks are more as you have nothing to lose.
8. It's not that there will be no hardships in the new venture. There will be, so be prepared to handle them.
9. At times, it may be difficult to take that major step towards your destiny. In that case, wait and watch and then act.

So, start now and take that very first step towards your destiny. Do whatever you feel is right. Thinking too much about the past and future will serve no purpose and only weaken your decision to start the new life waiting for you.

III. Follow Your Passion

> *What you seek is seeking you.*
> — *Rumi*

You should always follow your passion, focus on it, and believe me, you'll touch the sky.

In my view, this is one of the most important factors to have a happy and fulfilled life. Nothing can be more frustrating than to do something you don't like throughout your life. And this is the one most important reason for a failed and frustrated life.

But this is also true that this phrase is easier said than done. Because of one reason or another, we find it impossible or difficult to pursue our passion / dreams and succumb to other responsibilities and liabilities of life. We need to earn money to raise our families and that may be the reason that most of us relate success with the amount of money we make. And in my view, it is not wrong, because money is a very important part of our life and many of our worries may be reduced if we are financially strong. But to relate money with success is not right, because success is a very subjective measure and instead of money, it should be correctly related to happiness.

So if I'm happy and satisfied with my life and my career, then I'm successful, even if I'm making less money.

I've seen some people who are courageous enough to follow their passion and choose that passion as their career and they seem much happier than all IITians, doctors or CEOs and other so-called successful people.

I'm not saying that one should not become a doctor or engineer, definitely you should; but only if that is your passion. Don't follow any stream if you are not convinced about it. Never ever try your luck in something you have no interest in or just because someone else is successful. Even if your parents try hard to convince you. Always remember that their dreams are different from yours, so stick to your dreams. Only if you are clueless or not sure about what you want to do with your life, you should follow your parents' dream, though I am strictly against it.

To follow your dream is not an easy task and for that you need to have a certain plan in your mind, or better still, on paper. As I've said this earlier too that your life is yours only. It's your child and no one can do justice to your kid's (here your life's) future, not even your parents.

So if you want to be successful in life you need to follow *your* dreams and this is that simple.

Here I remember the story of a girl who was very focused from her childhood. She decided during her childhood itself that after 10+2, she was going to do her graduation in commerce, that too from SRCC, Delhi, which is a college of great repute. After completing her graduation, she would work for two years and after that she'd appear for an entrance examination for her MBA. You won't believe that she did exactly that and got selected into IIM, Ahmedabad and completed her MBA from there.

However, not all of us are so focused and many times we get confused with so many options available.

So how can we clear our mind to fulfill our dreams and follow our passion to make it big in our life?

According to my view, the following steps can be taken to do that:

1. Introspect and ask yourself repeatedly what you enjoy most in life since your childhood or is there anything you do during which time just passes in seconds.

2. If you have got your answer then the second step is to do a survey about your passion. What is the scope in that field and how much competition is there in the market.

3. Just keep in mind that those fields where there is more competition or no competition at all are not good options to follow.

4. But again, I must say that follow your instinct and if you believe in your dream, then nothing should stop you.

5. If you have decided your career, then half the battle is won, because the most difficult part of our life is to take good decisions.

6. Now you need to work on your passion because merely having a passion or dream will not take you there; you need to work hard to be successful.

7. If you have some unique ideas about your passion, then you are fortunate and you should apply those ideas to get the best result.

8. But if all your novel ideas are already taken up, which is a great possibility, then you need to think about something else.

9. If still you are not getting any new idea, then you can try the old ones, but with a difference. Anything which is done differently and interestingly may give you good results.

10. After deciding everything, start working on your dream. If you want a new skill, learn it now. Any instrument, marketing strategy or any new idea you need to implement, focus on it.

11. In the beginning, don't look for money, but instead focus on quality and try to build your brand. Because once your brand is formed, money will naturally come in.

So that is how you can focus on your dream, work on it and become successful in life.

Part B:
Other Factors beyond Control

A. Other Fish in the Sea

If your life was meant to be controlled, it would have come with a remote.

Just now I realized that it is very easy to say that you have to love your life just the way you love your child. But what if you have to deal with a difficult mother / father of your child? In other words, the other controlling factors of your life like your parents, your spouse, or your partner may have to be dealt with. If they are supportive, then your life can blossom like a flower.

But what do you do if they are control freaks and want to control your life according to their ways?

No wonder that this scenario can lead to a difficult life which may be filled with a lot of hurdles. Forget about loving your life, sometimes even to live your life normally may seem impossible. This is the time which gives you those moments of despair in which you may lose control over your life.

So what is the strategy to deal with such people?

1. First you have to realize that this is your life. Period.
2. Ask everyone to stay away unless you know that the other person is your true well wisher.

3. It's better to face criticism once, rather than face stress, failure, unhappiness every day, again and again.

4. If they don't listen, then you also start controlling their life. Very soon they will realize their mistake.

5. The more stubborn they are, the more aggressively you'll have to deal with them.

6. People will mock you, and bitch about you for your aggressive behaviour. Don't give them a chance again by responding.

7. In extreme cases, chances are that your relationships may end, and in such a scenario, you have to weigh both in terms of importance and then decide your next plan of action.

8. Many times people love to give advice, and only advice. In such cases, take things in your stride and do what you feel is right.

9. If you listen to those who only talk and don't act, they will be encouraged and will try to control you again.

10. If nothing works, take professional help.

This is a known fact that people try to control the lives of those who they think are soft targets and whom they can suppress or control easily. Here I don't mean that you should become a difficult person, but I simply mean that you need to show them that you are capable of handling your life and you want to live your life on your own terms. Because that is your life, your child, and no one else has the right to control it on your behalf.

I remember a story of my colleague during my first job. We all were very young and my colleague was married to a young, dynamic man who also worked in the same institute. In no time we became good friends and started sharing our feelings. My colleague Sujatha was a very good lady but always remained suppressed in presence of her husband. She was very lively and sporting otherwise, but when with her husband, she was completely different. Her husband used to criticize her for everything – her dressing sense, her looks, her profession and so on and that resulted in a lack of confidence in her. I knew that she was not happy in this relationship, but she never wanted to opt out of it. And if she was not willing, we could offer no help either.

We parted ways after some time when I moved to another city. After few years, I again got a chance to see Sujatha and when I saw her this time, she was completely changed from her earlier version. I was seeing a confident, well groomed lady, in place of that docile, humble girl who always had doubts about herself. Then she told me the tragedy of her life. Her husband had met with an accident two years back while driving under the influence of alcohol. He was in a coma for almost three months, which was the most difficult phase of her life. Her prayers and hard work didn't pay well and her husband succumbed to his injuries. After the demise of her husband, she was completely devastated for a few months. But for the sake of her daughter, she rose again and this time with much more strength and courage. And perhaps that was visible in her attitude towards life.

I agree that she had to stand up again for her child, but the change in her attitude was largely due to the absence of the controlling factor, which in this case was her late husband. He was so fond of controlling his wife and his daughter's lives that he forgot that they also had their own likes and dislikes. Had he respected their needs and wants earlier, they might have been living a much more fulfilled and content life from the beginning itself.

Now being the only one to handle her life, she was at ease with herself as well as her life. She was the only one responsible for her life as she was responsible for her daughter. As you can see here, whether it's her life or her kid, she needed to control it, love it and balance it with a simple act of authorizing and empowering it.

You can see here how the removal of one controlling factor can change your personality completely. And this is only one example; there can be hundreds of examples like this.

However, sometimes you 'yourself' can ruin your life. Yes, that is absolutely true. There are hundreds of examples where people themselves become the greatest enemies of their lives. They take terrible decisions in their lives which they know may lead to a miserable life, but they still do. They cannot stop themselves and give in to temptations, leading to complications in life.

I knew Sonali from my childhood days. She was a very docile, humble and simple girl. I really liked her a lot as a person. After she got married to a nice guy, she moved to another town. We were out of touch for almost nine years. And I really got a shock of my lifetime when I got to know that she had been arrested on the charges of her husband's murder. I couldn't connect the links which could have led to any conclusion. For me, she could never do such a heinous crime. But she was repeatedly shown on every news channel, crying hysterically and denying the allegations and I believed her fully.

But there were some unanswered questions. Who did kill her husband? Why was Sonali arrested? What was the motive of murder?

I was upset for almost two weeks and I really wanted to know the truth. I had full sympathy with Sonali, so I decided to visit her parents' house who lived in the same city.

When I reached, the ambience there seemed quite normal. They were least bothered about Sonali, rather they were focused on discussing the future of her twelve-year-old son, Mihir. I too met him and tried to get to know about Sonali a little bit and whatever I got to know through Mihir and others was even more shocking.

I could never imagine Sonali to be having an extramarital affair and that too with her brother-in-law. He played with Sonali's feelings and she was foolish enough to give in to the temptations. She could have fought off these temptations, but she gave up and thus made hers as well as others' life hell.

And I have derived a conclusion after seeing this and many such stories, that only a person who doesn't know her/his worth, will give in to such kind of temptation. These people give others so much importance that their little concern or attention is more than enough for them to surrender, and that inevitably results in all these complications. You can say here that due to low self esteem, these people may become weak in such scenarios.

Temptations are those road blocks which can block your journey to the right path and turn your life to some strange path. This may be extremely complicated, giving you lot of stress, anxiety and depression. And more often than not, it becomes difficult to return to your righteous path.

That's the reason we should strictly refrain from temptations which may give us short term pleasures but have long term complications and side effects.

B. Bonding with a Difference

> *There are no perfect relationships. It is how you accept the imperfections that makes it perfect.*

This is again an important part of life. As we all know that man is a social animal, so it seems natural that we need others to make our lives complete and worth living. All of us are surrounded by people who are associated or attached to us in some way and whatever we do in our lives revolves around them.

When it comes to relationships, every relation is important. Though it is also true that all people are not well wishers, and many of them may give us happiness at times while stress during other times. But it is also true that maintaining a relation is not an easy task. It is always easy to break or let go of any relationship, but difficult to hold on. It needs a lot of patience, perseverance, acceptance as well as selflessness to lead a good life with good people around.

In my view, two things should always be kept in mind while dealing with any relation or person:

1. Always treat the other person in the *same way* as you yourself wish to be treated by them. Here you have to show the same respect, love and compassion, which you want from them.

2. Always remember that there is a very fine line between every relation. This line is drawn by both persons who are in that relationship and one should never cross that line, under any circumstance. For some relations, this line/limit comes very early, which mean that the threshold is too close and these types of relations need extra care. While in others the threshold may be wide, and these are the relations where you can be more open as well as more tolerant towards each other.

If we follow these two rules, then chances are that we can maintain most of the relationships, though in a few cases you have to make extra efforts. But you have to keep in mind that in such cases, it's not always possible to succeed, as the other person's will to remain in that relationship with you is equally important.

The most easy and important way to deal with people is to prioritize them. Among family and friends, for example, you can choose family first, then in the family too, you can choose the one who requires you most at that time, like your little kid or ailing parents.

When you are going to prioritize your relations, be wise to differentiate between true well wishers and others.

This is not that difficult at all and you need to remember the following tips:

1. First of all, see whether you really like a person or not? Are you comfortable in their presence? A true friend will do everything to make you comfortable, so look out for that.

2. Secondly, in case of a new acquaintance, what do other people think of that person also matters. However, never judge a person by others' views, but try to find out the truth.

3. All relations are in reality based on the theory of give and take. This is a harsh fact of life that except for a parent-child relationship, almost all relations are run by needs.

4. A person who always talks about himself/ herself and never pays heed to your problems can never be a true friend. So, accordingly, you have to manage every person whom you come across in your life.

5. Never make the mistake of giving more importance to your relatives (except parents, siblings and offspring) than your friends. A friend will always win in such a scenario.

6. A person who always says, "Yes, you are right" to you is not right for you.

7. A relationship based on money will never last. Similarly, if money matters more in a relationship, it won't work.

8. In a relationship, you have to give your love and affection first and then you can expect something in return.

9. In a true relationship, you'll get a lot more satisfaction and happiness in giving.

10. Your self-worth and self respect are above all relations. Try to maintain that.

11. Last but not the least, sometimes when in doubt, listen to your heart; it is mostly correct.

In my own view, every person may be good for someone and bad for others. Depending on circumstances, we all behave differently with every person. It is simply because our behaviour is the reflection of the other person's behaviour with us. In other words, you can say that it is based on an 'action-reaction' theory.

I will react to your actions and vice versa.

You have to read the actions of others and your reactions as well. Try to stop if you think you are overreacting and try to stimulate yourself if you think that you are not reacting to a situation at all. Because by doing so you may really lose some good people in your life.

You need a certain outlook to pick those rare gems who can fill your life with happiness and contentment.

So, go ahead in the quest of such people.

III. Authorize your life

> *Start shaping your own day. Start walking your own walk. This journey is yours, take charge of it. Stop giving other people the power to shape your life.*
> *– Dr Steve Maraboli*

And I would say that these are the exact words I would like to use. In fact, if you look into it deeply, you will realize that throughout your life, you have only two persons that are solely yours. In other words, there are only two persons who you own and have complete authority over. And these are:

1. Your life, and
2. Your child (till he grows up)

And thus, just the way you deal with your kid, you have to deal with your life as well.

When you have complete authority over your life, you develop some responsibilities towards it, to make it as well more fulfilling. What are those strategies which you want to incorporate into your life to make it more content and blissful?

The first step towards it is to take charge of your life. Be responsible, be accountable and be answerable to yourself for all your decisions and all the steps taken. Ultimately, your life will be the way you choose to live and if you are satisfied and happy with what you have chosen, then the purpose of your life has been achieved.

If you authorize your life, it will definitely blossom like a flower because you feel that sense of responsibility towards it. This is a very simple yet universal truth about humans that when we possess something, we take great care of it. We don't want to lose it because we have a sense of authority and power over it. We seldom care for the things that belong to others.

In other words, take charge of your life as you do with your kids. You take complete responsibility of your kids' smallest needs. Similarly, there are a few needs and requirements of your life too, which you are supposed to fulfill. By doing so, you start taking responsibility of your every action, and at the same time, you stop blaming others. Believe me, this is an absolute necessary exercise to do because no one is responsible for your life, but you.

Every person in his or her lifetime makes uncountable mistakes, and it is very human to do so. What we are supposed to do is learn from these mistakes. Escapism and blaming others are negative traits which will never make your life better, but surely will make it bitter.

Now there are certain points which can help you to achieve this:

1. Take charge of your life.
2. This is not easy initially. To begin with, try to think twice before you act in any scenario.
3. Ask yourself what you would do if your kid was in the same situation.
4. Try to remain well aware and attentive when taking big or small decisions of life.
5. Try to improve yourself in various areas which can help you to take good and rational decisions regarding your life.
6. When you are satisfied with all your research and other factors, only then take the decision.
7. Always be sure that after so much work and research, it is unlikely that your decision will be wrong.
8. But… you know that destiny is always greater than your plan. So be prepared for unforeseen results which may turn out to undesired ones.
9. In that case, take full responsibility for your decision and never blame others for the results.
10. Try to find out the reason for your failure, work on it and then start again.

You can see here that when you take charge of your life, it is easier to manage it. You are the only one who is answerable to any questions raised by *yourself*. The other benefit of this is that no one else will try to plan your life according to them. People will know that your life is a very serious matter for you and you will never accept any interference from them.

Here I don't mean that you should not take suggestions or advice from others. You can always take the help of those who are true well wishers. There are always chances that many a time your true friends may see the problem more rationally. You being in the problem may face a blurring of vision as well as blurring of thoughts. So there is no harm in taking the help of others, but you have to draw a line and also have to be very careful while applying their ideas or suggestions, because whatever the other person is telling you, may not apply to you. Their intention may be right, but you have to learn to differentiate the needs of your life from theirs.

I remember the time when I was trying to plan a family. I consulted a local doctor, who was a gynaecologist from a suburb in India. My parents and a few friends who live near Delhi, asked me many times to see a good gynaecologist in Delhi itself. But I refused. My gynaecologist was very skilled and efficient, but just because she was practicing in the suburbs, I didn't consider her less skilled or less capable. I continued with my faith in her and finally I was blessed with my son. I firmly believe that it was her capability and my faith in her and in the almighty which fulfilled my dream of being a mother. But at the same time, it is also true that I didn't follow the advice of my parents and friends and I myself took charge of my life. Here I don't mean that their suggestion was wrong, but the simple reason is that they can't understand my life the way I can.

And this is only possible when you take charge of your life and know what is good or bad for you. When you learn this, you will own your life.

IV. Speak up and Emerge from the Cage

> *Every word has consequences. Every silence, too.*
> – Jean-Paul Sartre

That is the one thing, I will always advise you to do. 'You won't get, until you ask' and how true this saying is. Here I am talking about everything – your problems for which you need some advice, suggestions, or any materialistic thing.

What you feel or think about your life or even about someone else, you should speak up. Just say it. Speak out your heart. Those who are close to you will never judge you and those who are not, will judge you anyway, whether you speak or don't. Though I'll advise you to share your problems with your close ones, but still you can always speak to anyone.

However, sometimes it happens that you don't want to share with your family and friends as 'one of them' may be the reason for your troubles. You know that to disclose that person's name may hit back on you only. In such a scenario, you may find solace in the strangers or some other people like your friend's mother, your teacher, your neighbour, anyone, who you think won't judge you but give you the solution and will help you come out of that situation.

So the question is – why should you speak up and what are the benefits?

A few benefits are summed up here:

1. The basic thing is that you'll get what you'll ask for. Well, most times, if not always.
2. The burden you feel when you are stressed out can easily be taken out by sharing your problems.
3. People who genuinely care for you will be able to understand you as a person.
4. At the same time, you can also understand others better.
5. Problems can be sorted out more easily.

Now the big question is, how should one speak about his or her problems? How should one proceed?

Here are few ways by which you can open your heart in front of others:

Assess the problem - A very important step indeed and vital to solve any problem. Assess your problem. Is there any problem in the first place? Or are you making a mountain of a molehill?

If there is a real problem, then how big / important is this problem? Do you really want to discuss it with someone? If yes, then you can go ahead.

You have to decide here as this is your life's problem. In other words, this is your child's problem and you have to think deeply about it before sharing with anyone.

Assess the person - So you have decided to go to someone with your problem and want to discuss it with that person. But have you properly assessed that person? Many times it so happens that we share our problem with the wrong person and later regret our decision.

So on what points can you assess that person?

a. How close you are with the person. The closer you are, the better to consult the person (except in few cases, as highlighted above).
b. How authentic or reliable the person is, in terms of integrity, seriousness, humanity and the like.

So, now you have decided to go ahead to that person with your problems.

But a word of caution here, that by doing so you are authorizing that person to take vital decisions of your life. In other words, you are asking them to take decisions for your child. So indirectly, you are saying that you are not able to handle your life thus asking for their help. Though there is no harm in it, but it just makes it more important to choose the person wisely.

Secondly, be prepared for any advice or suggestion from the other person that you may not agree with. At the same time, a good amount of criticism may also come your way. But never lose heart because only a true friend or well wisher will tell you about your shortcomings or mistakes. Try to find them out, accept them and promise to work upon them.

However, sometimes you may not take criticism sportingly as you are already very disturbed due to the problem and it is really disheartening if someone accuses you and considers you responsible for the problem, even if they are right in their assessment.

With the double dilemma (one is the problem itself and other is the criticism), a certain kind of depression may set in which may be difficult to deal with.

In such circumstances, try to maintain your life's balance by following these rules:

1. **Share your feelings/thoughts** - As I said earlier, that is essential to do indeed. You have to talk to someone about your fears, your problems and why they are leading to depression? Are these thoughts worth your attention or tension? You need to talk about it. Sometimes another person can assess our situation better because we see the problem from inside, and may not be able to see it as a whole. The other person may give you better solutions as he is assessing the problem completely, including the causes and consequences. The only thing you have to keep in mind is that you have to choose your friend wisely. Choose those people who are non-judgmental and good listeners.

2. **Thought shifting** - This is the most important thing to do in any unfavourable circumstances. As we have already discussed, shifting of thoughts from negative to positive is the key point here. The only thing you need to do is completely ignore negative thoughts. Even if you have to push them out of your mind, do so and fill the gap with positive thoughts. Any thought, and I mean any thought, making you happy is a positive thought. Ponder over these positive thoughts till the time you feel better. The time when that feeling of worthlessness fades from

your mind, is the time, you know that you've won half the battle.

3. **Paradoxical thinking** - It is basically any thought coming to your mind, which is completely opposite of your current situation. For instance, after losing someone, you may want to be in another relationship, or after failing in a business, you may want to get a new haircut or something like that, which is not related to your problem, nor is a solution to it, but makes you happy. Go for it as this can be very helpful in acute situations and may act as a great therapy for depression.

4. **Take a deep breath** - Deep breathing exercises are worth mentioning here. They take nothing, but at the same time, make you ready to face the problem with more energy and more positivity. It is better to hold the deep breath for a few seconds for a quick and better result.

5. **Go for an outing** - Well, if you can, please do it. I understand that this is not easy, but do it if you can and by doing so, you can look at life with a different perspective. You can see that other people are suffering too and the grass is not greener on the other side as it may usually seem. If others can manage their life and their problems, so can you.

6. **Give a damn about what others think** - Well, you have to do this if you want to survive in this ruthless world. What others think about you or your life is none of your business. In fact, they will think or talk about you because they find you better than themselves. So instead

of feeling depressed about their views, you should feel good about the attention you're getting.

7. **Make god your companion** - Learn to walk alone and you will end up walking with god. This is true, just try it once. You have to believe in his existence and you will realize that you are *never* alone.

So be with you, be with him.

Personally I feel that the person, to whom you are going with your problem, should be wise enough to not discuss your mistakes. However, sometimes it becomes mandatory to reveal one's mistakes and if it is so, then you have to bear with it. Open your eyes, accept the truth, and move ahead.

Part C:
Odds of Life

The very next day, I went to Dr Aditi's place just to show her the manuscript I had written based on her life, her ideology and her viewpoint.

I must admit that in the last few months I had learnt a lot from her and my perspective towards life had changed a great deal.

- Now, I don't get irritated so easily.
- I have learnt to let go of things which are not in my hands.
- I know the power of positive thinking now and have learnt to see the blessing in almost every situation.
- I've learnt to accept things the way they are.
- And a lot more, I've incorporated in my life too.

That way, I've become more balanced and that has resulted in a calmer and happier version of me.

For me, it was a beautiful journey that resulted in a greater version of me and that was the reason that I wanted to share these ideas with everyone in the form of a book.

As soon as I entered her house, I felt the same aura but with a bit of difference. I could feel something amiss.

In no time her home manager came and greeted me with a cheerful smile. She made me comfortable and asked me to sit and went inside to call Dr Aditi. After a few minutes, Dr Aditi entered the room.

We exchanged greetings in the usual way. Though she was smiling, I could sense the lack of usual warmth in her greetings.

After we settled down on the sofa, I could feel the killing silence in the room for the next couple of minutes. For the first time in these months, I felt that awkwardness where two persons are sitting but none of them can utter a word.

Finally, I decided to break the ice, "What happened? Is everything okay?"

She just responded as if she had woken up from a deep sleep, "Yeah... All is well," she said and tried to smile.

"Okay, but why do you look so upset then? Is something bothering you?" I asked with genuine concern.

"No, it's not that, but I'm worried about Aarav," she finally spoke up. "Aarav has changed a lot. Now he doesn't listen to me anymore. Many times I feel that I'm not connected with him at all. It seems as if he is not my son but a stranger to me, and it bothers me," she said in a low voice, gazing at the wall.

"I understand, and sometimes, I feel the same about Arya. May be it's their growing age and they want some space now," I tried to console her.

"I agree that he needs space, but it's not about his space or freedom. It's more about my connection with him. It's about my existence in his wide and weird world." She said in a cracked voice and looked really disturbed.

I was a little confused and could not understand how to tackle the situation.

"I think you need to rest, Dr Aditi." I smiled forcibly. "This may not be the right time to discuss all these things. You and Aarav need some time to resolve the issues and to understand each other better. I take your leave now. See you later." She said nothing and I left.

On my way home, I was thinking about her. What I had seen that day was a completely new person to me. I'd seen a very vulnerable, disturbed and human Dr Aditi in place of the usual cheerful, strong and very balanced version of her.

The fact that she could be so weak and vulnerable, was still haunting me. I was going to write a book on her ideology, but she herself looked so disturbed. I started having doubts about my decision now. For the first time, I felt distraught.

As soon as I reached home, I just had a light dinner with Arya and Nikhil and went to bed. Nikhil asked me about my visit to Dr Aditi, but I refused to discuss anything and went to sleep.

The next morning, when I woke up, I was no better than the day before. I had a severe headache. I could not figure out what was wrong with me.

Nikhil, then, shouted from the kitchen, "Would you like to have a cup of coffee?"

I was so delighted to hear his voice, "Yes, I surely do!" I too shouted in a relieved tone.

After few minutes Nikhil entered the room with two cups of coffee. He sat beside me and started observing me.

"Hey, why are you staring at me?" I asked as I felt conscious of his piercing eyes.

"I want to solve the puzzle going on in your mind," he smiled and continued, "Tell me, what happened yesterday? Why do you look so disturbed dear?"

I too wanted to share my dilemma with him, but could not gather enough courage, as the fear of seeming stupid was bothering me.

"Where is Arya?" I asked him.

"He is still sleeping. Today is Sunday, you've forgotten." Nikhil smiled again.

"Oh yes, I forgot," I replied.

"So, can you now please tell me what happened yesterday?" Nikhil asked again.

Then I decided to share my thoughts with him and told him everything about Dr Aditi's reaction, my thoughts and my fear regarding seeing my ideal in her.

After hearing everything in detail, Nikhil became quiet for a few seconds while I eagerly waited for his response.

"Okay, now I'll ask you one thing. How would you react if you were in her place?" he asked.

I could not answer immediately because I was not prepared for such a counter question. "I don't know. May be I could have responded in a different way," I replied.

"What do you mean by a different way? See, you are disturbed because you have imagined her as a superwoman who can solve any problem. Right?"

"Yeah, it seems so," I said in a thoughtful voice.

Nikhil smiled and said, "And that is the cause of your worry. Why do you believe that Dr Aditi is any different from you? Just because she has survived so many tragedies in her life doesn't make her superhuman. She is just like you, me or any other human on the earth. You have made her your ideal because you like her as a person. She never insisted you do so, right?"

"Yeah." I was now getting the point. It was all woven by my needles of thoughts and so much so that it had become entangled in my own mind.

"As you know life throws many bouncers to us and we all need to face them. It's not about behaving in a particular way during those times as we all can behave awfully wrong in acute situations. But it's about coming out of those situations," said Nikhil.

It was a great effort put in by Nikhil to detangle all those silly thoughts. I thanked Nikhil for taking me out of that situation.

He smiled again and encouraged me to go for my next meeting with Dr Aditi, "Moreover when you meet her now, she will again give you a surprise."

"Really? How do you know?" I asked in a cheerful voice now.

"From your narration and description of her, I know that she is a fighter and survivor. She must have overcome her weakness by now and you will see her now in her old avatar," he said.

And I certainly could not agree more with him.

"Okay dear, now I have to go for my morning walk," Nikhil got up and left.

As soon as he left, I was again surrounded by my chains of thoughts. I analyzed myself and now really felt ashamed of myself. How could I think about Dr Aditi in that way? I just convicted her guilty for no reason and really made a mountain of a molehill.

Now, though I was feeling guilty, I felt better because my faith in myself and in Dr Aditi was regained. Now I didn't have doubts about my decision anymore.

I called Dr Aditi to set a new date and time for our next meeting. She was busy so couldn't pick up the phone, but her manager, after consulting her, told me to come over that evening.

I was looking forward to seeing Dr Aditi again after thinking so much about her.

As soon as I reached, I found her sitting in the drawing room.

"Hey dear, how are you?" she almost screamed excitedly.

"I am good, Dr Aditi. What about you?" I asked her.

"I'm perfectly alright." She laughed.

And I could see that Nikhil was absolutely right. I was really surprised seeing her so cheerful, calm and balanced again. She was now her usual self. And I was really happy to see her in her old avatar.

We sat down, and after a few pleasantries, came to the main point – the manuscript.

Though we were discussing the book, my mind wanted to know how she had overcome her fears. How did she manage to be normal again?

But it didn't seem right to ask her about that, so I kept mum.

Dr Aditi was observing me closely and she must have read my mind, so suddenly she asked, "You know what happened that day after you left?"

"No, how would I know?" I replied as if I had been caught red-handed.

"Yeah, how you would know." She smiled and continued, "After you left that day, I was still very upset. Then I made a cup of tea for myself and sat down in the garden all alone. I asked myself two things:

1. What is the problem?
2. What can be done to deal with it or what is the solution?

First, I assessed the problem and that was my son's behaviour. So I did a detailed analysis of his behaviour and observed two things:

1. Though Aarav's attitude had changed but when I compared him with other kids of his age, then he is still the best mannered and obedient child.
2. I, myself was responsible for the not so desired outcome for the two reasons:
   One, because of my not so modern thinking or you can say, conventional thinking, and second is, my impulsive response to his small mistakes which make them seem too big.

Keeping this assessment in mind, I concluded that first it's me who needs to change and then only I can ask for improvement in Aarav. From that day, I started working on myself and now I have seen great improvement in Aarav's behaviour and I'm really happy about that."

I could see the excitement and happiness in her eyes and at the same time felt really proud of her. How easily she had been able to analyze her mistakes and had tried to rectify them too.

She continued further, "You won't believe that many a time life too behaves in the same way. It seems that it is slipping from your hands just like sand and you have no control over your life. Life sometimes seems to behave like an autonomous body, which has no connections with you. It behaves in a manner that is completely strange to you and I call those phases the 'Odds of Life'.

"These are those instances which may show paradox or much unexpected outcome. And you may become totally in awe of it. Whatever you may call it, this happens with most of the people. I agree that these phases may be difficult to handle, but at the end you'll learn something. Sometimes life's wisest learning may come from these odds of life," she continued further.

As I wanted to know more about these odds, I asked Dr Aditi to explain them to me in detail. Then she narrated few instances of her life and a few of others around her. She tried really hard to make me understand what she meant. I understood after hearing all those stories that she wanted to tell me about those phases of life where the outcome is somewhat unexpected or unwanted. These phases of life are difficult, but when you look back, you may find some of them funny too. And that was the reason that she called them the odds of life, which means that something different will surface rather than the usual / expected outcome.

I asked Dr Aditi what we were supposed to do in such phases of our life.

"Well, sometimes too much is needed from us and sometimes we can do nothing. These phases of life show that life can behave like a stubborn child too. It may become totally unreasonable and unresponsive. In fact, these are the phases of life which appear as closed doors, but in reality, they will lead us to another door. And believe me, this door leads you towards a more fulfilling and purposeful life."

I understood all her points and asked her if we should include these odds in the book too and she said, "Why not! After all, these are practical lessons which we all learn from life and everyone should know that they are not alone facing all these odds, but others too are having the same experiences."

So here are a few important odds of life which I guess are experienced by all of us in some way or the other. Some of these may require some active action from us while others may not.

I. When you are about to quit, you'll get it

It's when things get rough and you don't quit that success comes.

This is by far the best quote I've read in the recent past, and surprisingly, this is the one saying, which, most of the time, turns true.

I am so sure about it because I've experienced this myself. The moment I feel that nothing can be done now, things start falling in place. It is as if god was waiting to hear my plea and then is ready to act swiftly.

I have seen so many instances of this in my life that I am a firm believer now.

I know an author who wrote two books, but both of them did not hit the market well. After that, he started thinking that writing was not his cup of tea. So he decided to quit. While he was in the process of winding up, he found an old journal lying around, totally unattended. He didn't pay any heed to it as he was totally shattered. After winding up he asked his wife to get the study cleaned while he went out for a walk.

The moment his wife entered the room, she laid her eyes on that journal. Curiously enough, she picked the journal and started reading it. As she read it further, she was empowered by shades of emotions. She wanted to smile at a moment and at the next moment her eyes would be wet. The journal contained their life journey which involved all the colours of life they had shared. She never knew that he had written such minute details of their life so beautifully in the journal. Their first meeting, first child, his first steps, how he got his first job and how he lost it in no time; every detail was present in the journal.

After reading a few pages, she decided to give it a shot and sent it to a publishing house.

Though it was not easy to do so and many publishing houses turned down that project, she rallied on and finally it was accepted by one. She was excited about the journal and thought that even if it didn't really do well, it would be a great gift for her hubby, their kids and herself.

To her surprise, as soon as the book hit the market, it was a huge hit. The readers were so moved by their story that the book became a huge success in no time. Her husband, the author, was overwhelmed by his wife's gesture and he dedicated the book and all the credit to his wife.

So you have seen with this example that most of the time, success is seconds away form the point we decide to quit.

So never quit and never give up because you never know when you are about to make it big. The mantra is to try, try and try until you get it.

The logic behind it may be of many kinds, but if I assess deeply, then a few can be illustrated:

1. By working on it meticulously, you have actually made things ready to happen and it's just a matter of time before it clicks.
2. For everything to happen, there is a time and place which is already decided.
3. According to the law of attraction, the more you want it, the more chances there are to get it.
4. When you are about to quit, you are very much depressed and in the deepest trauma, and when you are deeply hurt, you are closest to god. And when you are closest to god, your plea is heard easily by him.
5. Every prayer that is coming directly from a sad heart is taken up as a first priority by god, and acted upon accordingly.

II. The Mind deals with one problem at a time

> *Problems are not stop signs, they are guidelines.*
> *– Robert H. Schuller*

I will say that this is a blessing indeed. Whether you have one issue or several issues, it is a basic truth that our mind deals with one issue at a given time. This is such a simple and wonderful rule of nature that belongs to humankind.

We can't fill our brain with various issues or worries at the same time. We have to empty our brain just to fill it with another one. In fact, I think that god has done this deliberately to make things easier for us.

But if I ask, why did god do so? I got a great answer, which is: solve your problems one by one. Isn't it simple?

Moreover, god has also prioritized our worries, so you will be most tensed over the most important issue first and will keep aside the less important one. In the same manner, you have to solve your problems on the basis of priority.

The most important and recent issue should be handled first and then those issues which are not that important, and hence not to be given priority.

But how will you do that? Or in other words, is there any planned way to work out the same?

These are few points based on my research:

1. Write down what is bothering you the most. This is your top priority or number one issue to be dealt with.
2. Accordingly, jolt down all the issues disturbing you.
3. While making your list, try to list them according to priority. But, at the same time, don't be very strict with it as it can hamper your flow of thoughts. Moreover, you can always change it later.
4. Now arrange them according to priority, if you hadn't done it before.
5. According to Stephen Covey, you can arrange your tasks in four groups-

- Most urgent and most important
- Most important but not urgent
- Urgent and less important
- Not important and not urgent

6. The issues which are important should be our top priority and even if something is urgent but not that important like a phone call, you can omit it and deal with it later.

7. You can see now that the issues that come under first two groups should be dealt with on an urgent basis while the rest of the things can wait.

8. In fact, you'll realize that the rest of the issues are just like thrash which were occupying your mind unnecessarily.

9. Delete all unwanted thoughts and worries from your mind as they are burdensome and are not part of your life.

10. Save the rest, save yourself and save your life.

III. Why we Fall in Hate?

The way we fall in love, we fall in hate too.

We fall in hate because we are humans. It is that simple.

The person you hate actually has greater power over you than the person you love. And this is simply because hate is a much stronger emotion. The moment we hate someone, our life begins to change.

Yes, that's true. The person we hate is so deeply incorporated inside our mind that we can't think anything beyond him or her.

It occupies our mind, our heart and our life for that matter, and we do everything in our life keeping that person in mind.

We want to teach him / her a lesson, to make him / her jealous because we want to prove ourselves right and that person wrong in everyone's eyes.

But why do we do so?

Why can't we ignore or keep aside those revengeful thoughts?

The answer to this question is the same as I've discussed earlier too. And it is about emotional baggage which comes along with hatred, and that is the reason I said that hate is a much stronger emotion. Though I agree that it does not always happen the same way, but most of the time, the route and path are almost the same. And even if you understand the side effects of it and want to throw away all those silly thoughts, it seems extremely difficult, if not impossible to do so.

So, what should be your action plan in such cases so that you can keep yourself away from such negative and destructive thoughts?

I have prepared a ten-step plan for that and I know that it will be easier to handle the situation if you follow this plan.

1. Ask yourself why do you feel this way towards a particular person? Is there any specific reason or have you heard about that person from someone else and made an impression on the basis of their opinion?

2. If you haven't experienced anything bad about that person but have heard a negative review from others, then you should close the chapter there and then. Never ever believe anyone unless you've faced the same.

3. If you have had any bad experience with that person, then try to find out if you are also responsible for the outcome.

4. If yes, then try to rectify your mistakes and remove all your ill feelings about that person from your heart.

5. In spite of it being none of your fault, if you've faced criticism or some ugly response, then you may be right about that person.

6. Still I would suggest discussing your feelings with some neutral person, because many times we may not be able to see our own faults.

7. If the third person has enough guts to tell you the truth, then do the exercise no. 4.

8. If, fortunately or unfortunately, you tend to be right, then try to confront that person once. Sometimes people do things unintentionally and without realizing how much it can hurt others.

9. If that person accepts his / her fault and apologizes for his / her behaviour, then consider yourself lucky and try to forgive and forget all the episodes and give him / her a fair chance.

10. If nothing works out, then bear with it. There are all types of people in this world and we have to deal with them all from time to time. It may be easy sometimes, but most of the time it is difficult and may even be impossible.

There are a few rules which can be applied in such a scenario:

a. Try to keep yourself busy.

b. If any thought of that person is bothering you, then try to ignore it.

c. Keep yourself busy with other thoughts which give you happiness.

d. If nothing works, then analyze those thoughts in detail. What is the thing disturbing you the most? Is there any solution? If yes, then apply that.

e. If there's no solution, then try to keep yourself calm by avoiding that person or keeping minimum contact with him / her.

f. Practice meditation, do yoga and pray daily to fill your mind with positive thoughts.

g. Last but not the least, don't discuss that person with anyone. The more you discuss, the more disturbed you will be.

IV. If god has not given you one thing, he will give another

God has it all figured out. He will make a way where you don't see a way.

Yes, this is very true and I'm a firm believer of this. I have seen many cases where a person is weak in one area but extremely bright and strong in another. There are people who have some physical deformity but they may be very strong mentally or emotionally. Or there are people who are very good in a particular task or subject, but extremely poor in something else.

The idea here is not to blame yourself for any of your shortcomings. You are the way god has made you.

I know a boy who is visually impaired, but he is an extremely talented singer and a wonderful person. Those who are close to him always discuss his songs and his personality rather than his so-called deformity.

Similarly, there is a boy who studies in my son's class, Shashwat. He is a brilliant child and loved by all his teachers, but his handwriting is very poor. And many times he and his mom have had to face embarrassment due to his poor handwriting. The boy also understands this, but can't help it. His mom also tried calligraphy classes and other ways to improve his handwriting, but in vain.

So, there are many cases which can show us that how true this saying is. The problem arises when we see only our shortcomings and make a negative image about ourselves. We cannot see our positive traits due to constant nagging or criticism.

So what can we do in such a scenario and how do we deal with such a difficult situation? There are things which you can do about it and if you follow them persistently, then they are a sure shot way to success:

1. First focus on all your negative traits which are described by others or for which you have faced constant criticism.
2. Are they really your negative traits according to you? I am asking this because what others think does not matter, but what you think matters most.
3. If you agree with their points, then surely you must do something about it.
4. So the first thing you can do about it is try to improve yourself if you can. For example, if the issue is small like poor handwriting and you can do something about it, then you must do that.
5. The real problem arises when problems cannot be modified or rectified. For example, blindness, short height or any other physical deformity. The problem

here is that these things are not in your hand and you can do nothing to change them.

6. At this point, just remember the above saying, i.e. if god snatches something from you, he will give you something else. Try to find that out.

7. Try to focus on your passions, or anything for which you have received any praise ever. Ask you near and dear ones what they like about you. If your passion and their likings are the same, then you're bound to feel good.

8. Work on it rigorously because this is what you will excel in. Do give your one hundred percent and prove yourself in everyone's eyes, including yours.

9. If you answer is a 'no' to the question in point no. 2, then I must say that you are the most courageous and self reliant person on earth. Despite constant criticism, if you have no doubt about yourself or your abilities, then you need no one. Yes, it's true. You are a self sufficient person. Only a little focus will act as a kick on your butt and you'll start moving towards your goal.

10. You know your self-worth; the only thing which is stopping you is criticism. Start focusing on what you have rather than what you don't possess. When you choose the right path and are confident about it, then you can do wonders. Stick to your ideas, come what may.

V. The More you Give, the More you Get

Don't expect to receive if you are not willing to give.

Again, this is my favourite quote. And the big question here is what are you actually *giving*?

Because, if you give positivity, you'll get it back, and if you give out negativity, you'll get back negativity only. And don't expect it otherwise because this is how it works.

You can't expect to harvest mangoes after sowing babul seeds. So it's really prudent to keep watchful eyes on what you are providing to others and what you really want from them.

Another interesting point here is that first you have to give, and only then you can expect something in return. And this is the big mistake we all make in our lives. We start expecting from others too early and are never ready to give for it.

We start thinking that because I'm suffering from this and that, so I'm a victim. And if I'm a victim, then it's but natural that everyone should help me in all possible ways.

This thinking is absolutely wrong because if you are suffering then it is solely your responsibility to deal with it and no one else is responsible for your problems. And when they are not responsible, then why should they do anything for you?

I understand that as a human being, we all should help each other in times of crisis, but we cannot and we should not force anyone to do that. Nor can we blame them if they can't help us because everyone is busy with their own responsibilities and priorities.

So when I say that the more you give, the more you get, I simply mean that choose wisely what you are giving.

In other words, we can say that start giving the same thing you want for yourself. For example, if you want respect, start giving respect, you want love, give love, you want money, start donating it, and so on.

The list is endless because our desires are endless too. These are attributes of our lives which are priceless. In fact, this saying is for priceless things only as all the other things we can buy anytime.

This seems so very simple that if we want respect we'll give respect and we'll get it. And most of the times it happens as we expect it to.

But sometimes it so happens that you are the one giving, giving and giving but not getting anything in return. And I've seen in some cases that one person has given everything to another person without getting anything in return.

And in that scenario, the person who is giving may come across as a big fool.

Although it may be true to some extent, but I don't think that that person is a fool who has committed a big mistake by doing so. In fact, I consider the other person as the defaulter.

And if I look deeply, then I think there are two types of persons who cannot acknowledge the efforts of others and so do not reciprocate their attributes or good deeds.

1. A person who does not have any feeling for you. In other words, you are nothing in his / her huge world, of ambitions and achievements as the person is busy enough fulfilling his / her professional or personal life's goals. You simply don't exist in his / her dreamy world and that is the reason that he / she cannot return your obligations.

2. A person who is cold or inhuman not to feel the warmth of your love, respect and affection. This person will notice all your efforts but will not acknowledge them, and thus will fail to reciprocate.

In both the above examples, can we scrutinize why do we get such a response?

The answer is very simple; because they didn't ask for it. They didn't ask for your love or affection or respect, then why should they reciprocate it? And this is a known fact that we don't value the things we get without asking.

So what should you do in such a scenario?

1. Give them enough love or respect, but maintain your self-respect too.
2. If you are not getting any positive response within a short period of time, then there is no point in lingering on it.
3. Stop showing them any gratitude and move on.
4. Many times, people realize the value of something after losing it.
5. So let them taste their losses too.
6. Most of the times when people know the worth of your efforts, they realize your value and they will change their attitude.
7. If the other person realizes his / her mistakes, then you can choose to remain in that relationship, as many times, people remain ignorant about your efforts.
8. However, sometimes people may pretend to remain ignorant because they take you for granted. Try to look out for such people in your life.
9. Tell them clearly that you know their intentions, only if you want to hear some clarification because you still want to maintain those relations.
10. Otherwise, stay away, and believe me, this is a much better option.

VI. You plan something, God has another plan

Always expect the unexpected.

Many a time we want something from life but life takes a turn in such an unexpected way that it becomes difficult to deal with. It looks like we are nothing but slaves of our life. But it's not true and we should not think that way. When we presume that our life is our kid, then we will never think like that.

When you raise your kid, you think about his / her future though you do not know anything about it in reality. And I've seen many parents or you can say that most of the parents nowadays say that their child is free to choose his / her path and they will stand firmly by their child's side.

Imagine if we can choose to think the same about our life.

What if we can give the same liberty to our life? Let it take turns and twists which are mandatory. Let us stand firmly by its side. If we can think in this way and if we accept all the unexpected twists with dignity, then it will never be difficult to lead a successful life.

Moreover, it's not always about bad things happening to our life; we also get good things proportionately. The reason that we only remember the bad things that have happened to us is that we don't value the good things in our life.

So the next time you see any unexpected turn in your life, think about these factors:

1. Every life on this earth runs in a full circle.
2. This circle is made up of all events, good and bad, in equal proportion.

3. However, the timing and place of all these events are different with every life. And it is quite possible that the moment you are happy for any reason, someone somewhere may be sad due to the loss of a dear one.

4. And that is the reason that we should never compare our life with someone else's at a given point of time.

5. Whatever phase of our life is going on, we should have rock solid faith in the almighty.

6. And believe me, this faith is a very strong support in your life and will help you sail through the toughest period of your life.

7. Whatever is god's plan for us, remember it is always better than our plan.

8. And that is the reason that I advise one to flow with life in the direction it takes you along.

9. If you try to flow in the opposite direction, you'll only fail.

10. Moreover, it will exhaust you with all your efforts put in the wrong direction, leading you nowhere.

Sometimes it is better to wait and watch and keep your faith intact. At this point I remember a few lines said by great poet Sri Harivansh Rai Bachchan ji:

Mann ka ho toh achchha,
Mann ka na ho toh aur bhi achchha,
Kyunki usme bhagwaan ki marzi hoti hai.

And god will never do anything to harm us. If we believe that whatever happens in our life happens for good, then everything is good. And this is in fact the best mantra to lead a happy and peaceful life.

So next time if anything happens unexpectedly, trust god, have faith in him and hold yourself tight, so that you cannot be broken.

A very good thing I've noticed about us Indians is that we believe in the theory of surrendering. A wife surrenders to her husband and husband to his wife and that makes the core of a family. Because the moment you surrender, you become stress free, as you surrender your worries and sorrows too. The moment you surrender yourself to god, the feeling is even better. Just try it once and you will never have those worries again.

Besides this, the same theory can be applied to not only big events, but even day to day tasks. You plan something and something else happens.

For example, the day we plan to finish our work early and leave early, due to some reason or another, we stick there for a longer time than usual.

Last summer we planned a short trip to a hill station during the vacations. We had to leave on Sunday as it was a half day in our clinic. Though, it is a busy day because people find it easier to consult a doctor on a holiday, we usually finish by 2 p.m. So we booked our flight tickets accordingly. We had to leave around 4 p.m. as the flight would take off at 6 p.m. But as luck would have it, we were stuck at work till 5 p.m. We were pretty sure that we would miss the flight, but fortunately, it was late by thirty minutes, and so we could board it at the last minute.

So, as I said earlier, we should flow with life and many times things which are not planned and never expected, turn out to be the best thing in our life. And that is what makes life a complete phenomenon.

VII. The more you Cry about it, the more it Happens

> *Any fool can criticize, condemn and complain - and most fools do.*
>
> *– Benjamin Franklin*

I have seen many people in my life who just do nothing but keep crying over trivial issues. For these people, every deviation from the normal is a very big problem. If their maid didn't turn up, or if it is raining while they are away from home, or if unwanted guests turn up, anything like that is a huge problem.

And sometimes I really want to tell them that while they are crying over trivialities in life, just think that someone somewhere might be diagnosed with cancer or any other deadly illness, or someone may have lost a near one, or someone may have had a tragic accident or someone is dealing with poverty or domestic violence. They should realize that these are the real problems and one should feel really blessed if they are not one of the above mentioned people.

These people should also understand that the more you keep talking about something, the more it happens.

The moment you complain that how overburdened you are with the work, you will get one more file to work on.

The moment you say that you are tired attending to guests, a few more will knock on your door.

The moment you say that this was the most expensive month, another expense in some form or the other will stand in front of you.

The more you cry about your not so ill health, the more illnesses you will face.

So the rule of thumb is not to cry over small things in your life. Obviously, if there are bigger issues, then this may not apply, but this is very true for the smaller issues, we deal with daily in our lives.

The single strategy which can help in quitting this habit is not to over think. Most of the time we give so much emphasis to the deeds or situations, that they can actually overpower us and we start making the situation worst by crying over them.

In other words, you can say that over thinking is this baseless way of thinking which leads us nowhere. Instead, it may make things worse when overdone. The more you analyze things, the more detailed dissection you will do resulting in baseless interpretation and speculation and this gives you enough material to gripe over.

VIII. Rejection is the first step towards Selection

Rejection is the first step towards selection. You have to take that first step, howsoever harsh it may be.

So, never ever be afraid of rejection and take rejection as a positive start because it means that the first step has been taken.

I have seen many cases in life where rejection did not hamper the passion and confidence of the person. In fact, any person who takes rejection as a challenge will definitely succeed in life.

And if we think about it, then few things are important:

1. As I've said rejection is the first step, so according to that, the process has been initiated.

2. If you are rejected and take it as a challenge, then you actually promise yourself that you have to succeed one day. And that promise is very important as it motivates you to work hard with full dedication and devotion, which ultimately leads you to success.

3. And not only that, dedication and devotion can make you a miraculous person and lead the way for you to see phenomenal success in the chosen field. And this is evident in many examples which resulted in super success of those great personalities who were once, twice or maybe many times, rejected.

There are plenty of examples from all over the world, but in India itself such people are no less in number.

Legendary Lata Mangeshkar, Amitabh Bachchan, Mary Kom, Asha Parekh... the list is endless.

Asha Parekh is a noted and successful actress of the yesteryears. And she herself narrated the story of her rejection. In a popular TV show, she narrated how she was cast in a film and also shot for the film for a few days. But later she was rejected by the film producers saying that 'she was not star material' and some other actress was selected in her place.

And you will be surprised to know that Asha Parekh later became very successful and a leading actress of her time while the actress who took her place in that movie couldn't make a mark in the film industry.

We have many examples like these, which teach us that we should never be disheartened by rejection, but should take it as a challenge.

These are cases where our hard work and perseverance could make the change which led to success. But what if rejection comes from someone special? In fact, many people think of rejection as a synonym to this.

And the real problem is that you cannot do anything about it because it is about someone's choice. And most definitely, you cannot change anyone's choices. But what can you do about the disappointment, frustration and worthlessness engrossed in your mind after the rejection?

The only answer to this is that you have to deal with it and I'll tell you how to do that.

1. First of all, it's about the person's choice as we discussed earlier, so don't bother about that too much; everyone doesn't necessarily make good choices.
2. Never ever should the feeling of worthlessness come to your mind because that person is not worth having you in his / her life.
3. You are precious and priceless and that is the reason that the other person can't afford you.
4. You are way ahead of that person, and to prove that, you need to work on yourself.
5. Keep yourself busy and move on because somewhere someone *'better'* is waiting for you.
6. Also give the benefit of doubt to the person because many times people behave in a certain way because of some reason we are not aware of.
7. Whatever the reason, stop thinking about that person and bury the harsh feelings you have for him / her.

8. This is important for the peace and well being of your mind.

9. Focus on yourself and do whatever you like and have longed to do in your life.

10. Give yourself time, because time is the best healer. Though I know that there are many wounds which stay in our hearts for our whole life and leave a scar, but their intensity is most definitely reduced with time and you can lead a normal life with the wounded and healed heart.

So keep working on it so that rejection can never affect you. Instead, it should result in a better and greater version of you.

IX. Feeling Entangled? Just Wait and Watch

Be patient. The best things happen unexpectedly.

Till now, we have discussed those phases of life where you have to do something. But now I'm going to tell you about the phase of your life where you need to do nothing. And believe me, this is true.

These are those phases of life where you find yourself entangled in a hundred thoughts and the work you have to do regarding that. You are so confused and worried that you don't know which step of yours will solve the problem and which step will land you in trouble. And this is the time you start doubting yourself and your capabilities. No one can help you, either because you are the one who can understand your situation and the dilemma caused by it.

So what can be done in such a scenario?

Nothing, practically *nothing*. Just go with the flow of life and do nothing. There are many phases of life which just come and go in the simplest manner. The more you put your efforts in it, the more complicated it gets. And the process which might have ended on its own, now requires not only you, but others too, to bring you out of this entangled state.

Many a time things fall into place by themselves and we need to do nothing. But the problem here is that even if I'm telling you to do nothing, you don't know how to deal with *yourself*. Your frustration, your worries, and your fears of the unforeseen definitely need to be tackled. I agree that this may be difficult initially, because you have to fight with yourself here. Your heart says that everything will be fine, but your mind is full of fears and that may result in a disturbed state of mind. So what can you do to maintain your peace of mind in this scenario?

You will see here that your effort and self-realization is needed in every phase of life. I'm saying here that you have to do nothing to solve the problem, but many of you may find even this theory a problem. Because it is very difficult to sit calmly and doing nothing in any turbulent situation. In such a scenario, just remember how you would behave if your kid behaves weirdly and refuses to take all your advises and suggestions? You will try to control yourself first to control the situation. Isn't it? So again, you have to put in an effort, not to solve the problem but to keep yourself controlled, calm and stress free, because your life is no different from your kid. Having said that, I agree that it is easier said and done.

So what can be the strategy to deal with yourself in such a situation?

The following are the tricks:

1. First you have to decide and convince yourself that this is the situation where you choose to do nothing.
2. This can be done by a thorough scrutiny of the situation.
3. Just tell yourself that you choose to do nothing, not because you don't want to do anything, but because you know the pros and cons of your decision.
4. And the same thing (point no. 3) you can also tell others, who are after your life, wondering how you can sit calmly in such a situation.
5. Repeatedly tell yourself that you are doing nothing wrong in doing so and whatever you are doing is the only solution to this problem.
6. Keep yourself busy in whatever ways you can. Go for a walk, watch TV or read something.
7. And yes, never ever discuss the problem you are dealing with. The more you discuss it, the more doubt you will have about your decision.
8. Track your problem off and on, just to see if the situation is improving.
9. Don't lose heart if you see no improvement in the situation. Often things take a sharp U-turn in no time, which may solve the problem.
10. Give yourself time and have faith in yourself, your capability and god.

Whatever is the end result, you have to bear with it. It may take years to solve, or it may be solved within seconds. So in the meantime, it would be a better idea if you have something else to keep yourself busy, calm and content.

X. The moment you get what you have longed for, you lose interest

Just like a child who wants a toy desperately, and as soon as he gets it, he loses interest in it and wants another toy.

And let me tell you that we adults are no different from children in this particular trait.

Things have value in our life in two situations:

- First, before getting it
- Second, after losing it

And this is the harshest fact of life, that we take things for granted most of the time. What if we realize that everything which we possess is precious too? Believe me, if we think that way, our life will be much more fulfilling. We will be having fewer desires, less jealousy and more happiness and satisfaction in our lives.

I have seen many girls during my college days who were wooed and proposed by many boys. But they refused their proposals seeking someone better. And when the other person moved on, they regretted their decision. And the reason why they did that is simply because they took them for granted.

Though in most of these cases, people may also be commitment phobic, and it may be difficult to indulge in any relationship.

But if we stick to the topic, then it is seen that we human beings lose interest in everything really fast – be it a book, a gadget, a toy, or even a person.

And that may be the reason behind so many failed marriages, which includes both arranged as well as love marriages. Because the moment you realize that now this person is your spouse, you start taking him / her for granted. You start finding faults and mistakes in everything and you start wishing for something better than what you have.

If you are thinking on the same lines, then let me assure you that you are no different from others and you are a perfectly normal individual. Because this is a normal phenomenon and we all are similar in our thinking.

But something cannot be right just because we all are doing it. So what is the right thing to do?

The right thing to do is:

To value what we possess.

And how can we do that?

We can do that by training our mind in such a way that it starts appreciating our possessions.

1. Make up your mind that you are going to do that and this decision in itself is the first key towards this program.
2. Once you've decided, start making a blueprint of your possessions which can include anything, but most importantly, people, including your spouse or partner.

3. This blueprint should include almost everything about your partner, i.e. positive as well as negative traits.

4. Now on a sheet of paper, write one negative point and cut it with one positive point. This way you have to neutralize every negative trait with a positive one.

5. There are chances that you find more negative traits than the positive ones. In that case, open your eyes wider and increase your field of vision to find more positive qualities.

6. When it comes to your spouse or partner, then let me tell you that the grass on the other side always looks greener, but you never know how much effort is needed.

7. So it is always better to water your own grass and put all the effort needed for it to grow.

8. Things look good from outside because you are not seeing everything it involves. In other words, you will find out many things about your partner once you start living with a person 24x7, and they could be both, pleasant as well as unpleasant.

9. We should also remember that any relationship depends on a give and take theory.

10. So, we should also study what we are offering to sustain a relationship. As said earlier, the more we give, the more we get. It is that simple.

And the same holds true for life too. It's your possession and you need to value it. Don't spend those precious years of your life carelessly because *you live only once*.

So try to make this 'one-time' a memorable one. Not for the sake of people, but for you – your happiness, your growth and fulfillment.

Your life is your child, your possession. So it is your responsibility to try to make the most of it. And how can you do that?

You can do that by following the plan mentioned in the book which teaches us to value our life. In a nutshell:

- By smiling often
- By forgiving others
- By accepting yourself with unconditional love
- By accepting others as they are
- By not expecting much from others
- By letting go
- By following your passion
- By giving more
- By counting your blessings. And…
- By expressing gratitude for everything you have.

An End is a New Beginning

Your life is your message to the world. Make sure it is inspiring.

"So finally, we are proceeding towards the end and I'm happy that we were able to put in this plan in black and white," said Dr Aditi with her usual cheerful smile.

"Yes, Dr Aditi. It's the result of the hard work put in by our efficient team and because of their efforts we are able to hold our project in hands." I too was very happy finishing our project. At the same time, I was overwhelmed and grateful for the inspiration and motivation I got from Dr Aditi's life. I wondered if we could have more ladies like her in the world, who can live their lives on their own terms, who can be a mother to their lives too and thus nurture their lives in a way they nurture their kids.

Though the end of the book has arrived, let's not forget that every end is a new beginning. This is the time to act, because you still have some part of your life which can be worked upon and made better than before.

So think about it; you are still alive and you still have your life. Believe me, it is still your child. Go ahead; start afresh with the practical and easy ways mentioned in the book. Do something today that your future self will thank you for.

So start now, make plans, and act now. Remember, you are unstoppable. So move, rather rush towards your goal.

Run… until you reach there. Run… because you haven't stopped yet.

"And it's not over, until you say it's over."

I could not agree more with these words of wisdom from Dr Aditi.

References

1. Holden, Robert. *Happiness Now!: Timeless Wisdom for Feeling Good Fast.* London, United Kingdom: Hay House, 2007.

2. Emmons, Rober A. *Thanks!: How the New Science of Gratitude can Make you Happier.* University of California at Davis: Houghton Miffin, 2007.

3. Carlson, Richard. *Don't Sweat the Small Stuff and It's All Small Stuff.* New York City, USA: Hyperion, 1996.

4. Eker, T. Harv. *Secrets of the Millionaire Mind.* New York City, USA: Harper Business, 2005.

5. Edelman, Ric. *The Truth About Money.* New York City, USA: Harper Business, 2010.

6. Achor, Schawn. *The Happiness Advantage.* Cambridge, United State: Currency, 2010.

7. Barrett, Sondra. *Secrets of Your Cells: Discovering Your Body's Inner Intelligence.* Sounds True, 2013.

8. Dooley, Roger. 'Why Faking a Smile is a Good Thing'. 26 February' 2013, www.forbes.com.

9. Grandy, Alicia A.; Fisk, Glenda M.; Mattila, Anna S.;Janeson, Karen J.; Sideman, Lori A. 'Is "Service with a Smile" enough?

Authenticity of positive displays during service encounters' *Organizational Behavior and Human Decision Process.* Volume 96, Issue 1. Pennsylvania State University, USA: Elsevier, 2005. January, pages 38-55. www.sciencedirect.com.

10. Dimberg, Ulf; Soderkvist, Sven 'The Voluntary Facial Action Technique: A Method to test the Facial Feedback Hypothesis' *Journal of Nonverbal Behavior.* Volume 35, Issue 1. Dept. of Psychology, Uppsala University, Uppsala, Sweden. 2011. March, pp 17-33. www.springer.com.

11. Giang, Vivian, 'How Smiling Changing your Brain'. 28 January 2015. www.fastcompany.com.

12. Routledge, Clay '5 Scientifically Suggested Benefits of Prayer'. 23 June 2014. www.psychologytoday.com.